GROWTH HORMONE:

REVERSING HUMAN AGING NATURALLY

The Methuselah Factor

GROWTH HORMONE:
REVERSING HUMAN AGING NATURALLY

The Methuselah Factor

James Jamieson and Dr. L.E. Dorman
with Valerie Marriott

*"The overall deterioration of the body that
comes with growing old is not inevitable...
We now realize that some aspects of it
can be prevented or reversed."*

– Daniel Rudman, M.D
New England Journal of Medicine

Published by J. Jamieson
St. Louis, MO 63108
USA

ISBN # 1-884820-30-1

Library of Congress Catalog Card Number 97-62105

Growth Hormone: Reversing Human Aging Naturally is not
intended as medical advice. It is written solely for informational
and educational purposes. Please consult a health professional
should the need for one be indicated.

Published by J. Jamieson
St. Louis, MO 63108
USA

CONTENTS

"This book fills a much-needed gap."

– Moses Hadas, in a review

Note to the Reader: The contents of this publication are for informational purposes only and are not in any way meant to provide medical advice. If you choose to use the therapies described herein, please consult a qualified physician to guide you in that process.

*"Everything has been figured out,
except how to live."*

– Jean-Paul Sartre

INTRODUCTION

Throughout recorded history, man has sought after the fountain of youth. Though we are still on that quest, the time has come that we understand many aging processes and how to control them. We know about the destructive effects of free radicals on our cells, and the importance of antioxidants in neutralizing this damage. Genetic research is unveiling DNA codes that predetermine our ability to rid our bodies of toxic compounds from our environment that may promote the growth of cancer. The most widely recognized and addressable influence on aging is the decline of hormone production that begins in the mid-thirties. We are familiar with the replacement of estrogen and progesterone in menopausal women, while recently testosterone replacement for men and women has become more widely accepted. Physicians are finding that when a wider array of hormones is replaced, patients attain much greater results than with any single hormone and, in some cases, one may protect against the side effects of another.

While the use of hormone replacement has advanced the field of anti-aging medicine, in common practice it is flawed. We need to question the ethics of using synthetic hormones as replacement rather than the natural ones that are cheaper, safer, and recognized by the body. Beyond that, we need to question what other anti-aging hormones are available, and if they too are declining, what advantages are there in replacing them to youthful levels? Can we go beyond preventing the symptoms of aging to turn back the biological clock? According to the studies on growth hormone, we can.

Perhaps one of the most interesting differences between GH and other hormones is that the body keeps making large amounts of GH right into old age, while other hormones diminish in their production. The challenge in restoring youthful levels of GH for most of us is not increasing our production or injecting the hormone itself, but releasing it from its sequestered state. We now know how to unlock the gates that keep GH from circulating in the body.

What is hGH?

Human Growth Hormone is one of many endocrine hormones, like estrogen, progesterone, testosterone, melatonin and DHEA, which decline with age. While many of these hormones can be replaced to deter some of the effects of aging, hGH reaches far beyond the scope of any one of these hormones

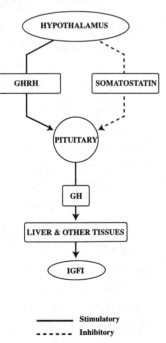

to not only prevent biological aging, but to significantly reverse a broad range of the signs and symptoms associated with aging. In effect, hGH therapy has been shown to turn back the biological clock by <u>20 years or more</u>!

hGH, also known as somatotropin, is the most abundant hormone secreted by the pituitary gland. It is produced at a rate that peaks during adolescence when accelerated growth occurs. Daily growth hormone secretion diminishes with age to the extent that a 60-year-old may secrete 25% of the hGH secreted by a 20-year-old. Growth hormone is primarily released in pulses that take place during the beginning phases of sleep, then it is quickly converted in the liver to its powerful growth promoting metabolite, Insulin-like Growth Factor type 1 (IGF-1)—also known as somatomedin C. IGF-1 elicits most of the effects associated with growth hormone and is measured in the blood to determine the level of growth hormone secretion. IGF-1 promotes glucose transfer through cell membranes as a source of fuel for cells, which is an insulin-like effect. Thus the term IGF-1, or insulin-like growth factor. Most of the beneficial effects of hGH that we will explore are directly associated with IGF-1.

The decline of growth hormone with age, sometimes referred to as somatopause, is directly associated with many of the symptoms of aging, including wrinkles, gray hair, decreased energy and sexual function, increased body fat and cardiovascular disease, osteoporosis, and more. Many of these symptoms have been associated with younger adults who have growth hormone deficiency; in a sense, the biological age of these adults has surpassed the chronological age. The good news is that clinical evidence demonstrates that by replacing growth hormone we can dramatically reverse these symptoms to restore hair color and growth, regain bone tissue, increase energy, and significantly reduce body fat.

Decline in Growth Hormone with Age

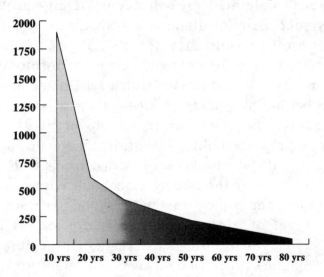

Why do hGH levels decline with age? Researchers have examined the evidence and some theories suggest that the effects of changes in GH regulating hormones like somatostatin and growth hormone releasing hormone (GHRH) account for GH decline. The encouraging evidence is that the aging pituitary maintains the ability to release growth hormone, if it is properly stimulated to do so. Proper diet, exercise, and secretagogues, when used correctly, allow the pituitary to significantly increase levels of growth hormone. Secretagogues are substances on the cutting edge of scientific research that stimulate the pituitary to secrete growth hormone; we will look at these materials in detail and examine the exciting clinical evidence that demonstrates how effective they are. We will also examine the relationship between diet, exercise, and hGH.

Until recently, growth hormone therapy has only been available in the form of injections that have been prohibitively expensive and difficult to use. Now, there are natural substances that have been well documented to stimulate growth hormone in a way that may exceed the effectiveness of injections or compliment injection therapy. According to researchers, these cutting edge natural secretagogues may have the ability to more closely mimic the body's youthful GH secretion patterns than any other therapies previously available.

"I am not young enough to know everything."

– Oscar Wilde

CHAPTER ONE

YOUNG AGAIN: HISTORY OF hGH, PAST TO PRESENT

In May of 1989, Daniel Rudman held the first of 12 syringes up to the light. Seated before him was a 73 year-old man. "Are you ready?" he asked his elderly patient. "Ready as I'll ever be," came the reply. The syringe contained a small amount of recombinant growth hormone dissolved in clear liquid. Rudman swiftly injected him.

Dr. Daniel Rudman was doing something never done before within the confines of medical research: he was giving perfectly healthy men a cloned version of what has come to be known as GH. Growth hormone is a hormone secreted in the brain by the pituitary. Everyone who ever attained normal height has it. Or — had it. GH levels drop off with age, and not so coincidentally, all the things that go with it become history as well: strength, muscles, energy, strong bones and teeth, thick skin, sex drive — that indefinable optimism of youth — gone. But what would happen if older people were given back their GH?

Four years before Rudman began his experiment, a very strange thing occurred at movie theaters across America. Next to the Rambo crowd were lines of white-haired moviegoers—some in wheelchairs, others leaning on canes. People who hadn't seen a movie in 20 years were waiting patiently to see a movie, which, by all accounts, starred bunch of old fogies. The movie was Cocoon, and it was Hollywood's incarnation of one of mankind's most persistent reveries: what if an older person could become young again?

Four years later, Daniel Rudman was making the first steps towards answering that question by injecting 12 people with growth hormone (GH). Fortunately for them, he was relying on Eli Lilly rather than alien pods to supply the solution. The preliminary data was in as quickly as it appeared in Cocoon; energy, vitality, endurance, sex drive, optimism and happiness all rebounded with GH.

Within 6 months, Rudman had the final data. In a strict scientific sense, his patients had become younger. Ten to twenty years of aging were peeled from their laboratory profiles. Their skin was thicker, muscles were bigger, age-related stomach fat was disappearing, and lost bone from the spine was

---

Effect of Human Growth Hormone on Lean Body Mass, Adipose (fat) – Tissue Mass, Skin Thickness and Bone Density in Healthy Men Ages 61-73

Lean Body Mass .... +8.8%
Bone Density (Lumbar vertebrae) .... +1.6%
Adipose-Tissue Mass .... -14.4%
Skin Thickness from 4 sites .... +7.1%

---

* Instead of measuring GH, scientists rely on IGF-1, which is provoked by GH and elicits most of the benefits associated with growth hormone. IGF-1 measurements are easier and much more accurate than GH measurement.

restored. Their levels of insulin-like growth factor (IGF-1*) had become equivalent to that of a 20-year old.

The first indication that earthlings might be able to reverse the aging process was published in the New England Journal of Medicine in July 1980, starring Dr. Rudman and his group of 12. Just as Hollywood producers scramble to imitate a box office hit, scientists all over the world began to assemble clinical studies that would eventually confirm Rudman's results and reveal new applications for growth hormone.

What Is Growth Hormone?

The discovery and designation of the term growth hormone was derived from its visible manifestations. Physicians had long known that there was a substance from the brain that made people grow. But it wasn't until 1912, that the eminent researcher and surgeon, Harvey Cushing, identified this elusive substance and termed it "the hormone of growth".

In 1956, endocrinologist Maurice Raben finally isolated "the hormone of growth" from human and monkey cadavers. In 1958, he advanced growth hormone research to the next level by injecting it into a dwarf child. As the child began to grow, the hormone finally lived up to its name.

The pituitary gland, which manufactures growth hormone, is located at the base of the brain, and GH is only one of many hormones it releases. GH production is controlled by its manufacturing cells called "somatotrophs", while its release is controlled by chemical messages from the hypothalamus. These important distinctions between GH and other hormones present options in treatment methods, which we will clarify in future chapters. Studies have clarified human GH releasing patterns, by measuring GH every 5 minutes for an entire day. It is released in four main bursts, or "pulses", in young men, while young women exhibit more frequent bursts that collectively represent 50% more daily secretion of GH. Most of the day's GH release occurs at night during slow wave sleep, and the remainder is released in smaller bursts during the day, which are often determined by exercise and dietary patterns. GH may be released about 12 times during a 24-hour period, but after the age of 50, the number and intensity of pulses is decreased. GH decreases about 14% every decade into old age to the point that some elderly people don't release any detectable GH at all.

GH has many effects in the body, and what it does may be best illustrated by what happens when it's not there.

Growth Hormone Deficiency

Children

In children, the effects of GH deficiency are easily discernible. Children lacking GH have short stature, small hands, feet and skull. Teeth are late in coming in, and skin is so pale that the veins show through. Nails don't grow, and the voice is high-pitched. Even little kids get the fat-around-the-middle that is so characteristic of GH deficiency in adults. In addition, their bones are porous and their lean tissue mass is reduced.

Skin

In adults with GH deficiency, the skin is thin and collagen deficient. Wrinkles known as "crow's feet" may be caused, in part, by GH deficiency. People who have had their pituitaries removed have pronounced "crow's feet". While the connection hasn't been absolutely proven, research has shown that GH treatment increases serum Type III procollagen—an important building block for skin and connective tissue. Decreased skin thickness and resultant wrinkles are signs of old age; increased skin thickness and smoother skin are evidence of GH treatment.

Dehydration

GH deficiency also causes dehydration and decreased sweating. People with GH deficiency can't tolerate cold and have difficulty cooling off during exercise. In short, these people cannot thermoregulate. Lack of hydration often becomes evident when blood is drawn; people with GH deficiency are often told by the phlebotomist that he or she "can't find a vein". Not surprisingly, GH-related dehydration is associated with kidney problems. Adults with GH deficiency have reduced filtration and reduced renal plasma flow. Age-related dehydration, or "shriveling up" of bones and skin, is largely caused by GH deficiency.

Heart and Exercise

Decreased blood volume due to dehydration may contribute to the heart problems experienced by adults who are GH deficient, but there seem to be other ways in which GH deficiency inhibits proper cardiac function. Atrophy of the heart muscle is an important factor. Studies suggest that GH elicits an anabolic effect on cardiac muscle. This is not surprising, given its effect on lean muscle mass. People with GH deficiency also have extremely reduced exercise performance. Maximal oxygen uptake (VO2 max) is only 70-80% of normal. It has been reported that this will reverse within three years of GH injection therapy.

Metabolism

Metabolism of glucose, protein, and fats is abnormal in GH deficient adults. Sugar metabolism and accompanying insulin resistance is a problem particularly in obese adults with GH deficiency. GH therapy has a known insulin regulating effect and often results in normalization of blood glucose.

Proper protein metabolism requires insulin regulation and other mechanisms, which are greatly improved with GH therapy. The benefits of GH in this area are evident in the increase of lean muscle mass due to improved muscular protein uptake.

Fats

Lipids are a real problem for GH-deficient adults. Total cholesterol, LDL cholesterol and apolipoprotein-B are elevated. HDL ("good") cholesterol has been reported in some studies to be subnormal. GH deficiency causes increased thickening and hardening of arteries, and increased plaque formation. These physical changes, along with the changes in blood lipid profile contribute to the increased risk of heart disease for GH deficient adults. Increased body fat, particularly in the abdominal area, is common in those who are GH deficient.

Psychological

Long term studies show GH deficiency to be consistently associated with extreme impairment of psychological well being. Patients in these studies typically exhibit similar symptoms, including lack of energy, optimism, and "zest for life". They are frequently "loners" who lack friendship, intimacy and career satisfaction. They report difficulty with memory, concentration, and motivation. They are frequently "in a bad mood", and depressed. Unfortunately, many of these people, including the elderly, are frequently mistreated with antidepressant drugs.

All of the symptoms of GH deficiency that we have described thus far were at first founded in their consistent association with low GH levels. These correlations were then substantiated by the reversal of these symptoms with the use of GH therapy. In chapter two, we will detail some of the studies that support these and other areas of therapeutic potential that growth hormone therapy has to offer.

CHARACTERISTICS OF GROWTH HORMONE DEFICIENCY

Anabolic Tone
Reduced lean body mass and/or skeletal muscle mass
Reduced skeletal muscle strength
Reduced exercise performance
Increased total body fat
Increased abdominal and visceral fat

Lipid Effects
Elevated LDL cholesterol
Decreased HDL cholesterol
Elevated apolipoprotein-B

Bone Effects
Osteopenia (lack of bone)

Metabolic Effects
Insulin resistance (in obese people)
Hypoglycemia
Possible abnormal resting metabolic rate
Reduced T4 to T3 conversion

Protein Synthesis
Thin skin
Lack of collagen
Decreased size of organs
Decreased nail and hair growth

Dehydration
Reduced glomerular filtration and renal plasma flow
Reduced sweating — inability to thermoregulate
Reduced cardiac output (potentially)
Increased vascular resistance

Mental Health
Reduced energy
Emotional instability
Poor memory and concentration
Depression
Lack of social interaction
Lack of purpose
Reduced Sex Drive

Adapted from Cuneo RC, Salomon F and PH Sönksen. The syndrome of growth hormone deficiency in adults. In Anders Juul and Jens O.L. Jørgensen, eds. Growth Hormone in Adults: Physiological and clinical aspects. New York: Cambridge University Press, 1996; 145-167.

Factors that Influence GH

Obesity diminishes pulsatile secretion of GH. It also causes accelerated breakdown of GH by the body. On the other hand, sustained high-intensity exercise increases the quantity and number of pulses of GH release. Intense is the key word here; garden-variety jogging won't do it.

Fasting increases both the pulsatile frequency and the amount of GH secreted. Eating shuts it down by stimulating insulin, which opposes GH. Over the long term, a poor diet can tremendously interfere with proper GH release and IGF-1 formation. The correct diet will assist in overcoming excess insulin in order to promote growth hormone. In chapter six we will detail diet and exercise routines that will help to optimize your GH release and response.

Testosterone, estrogen, and other hormones enhance GH secretion. The synergistic effect of replacing a variety of deficient hormones cannot be overstated. Results in this area are enhanced with the use of the proper forms of these hormones that are recognized by the body. In chapter seven we offer some guidelines for understanding the role that various hormones play in GH management.

The amino acids L-arginine and ornithine can cause GH release if taken in high enough amounts. Certain drugs also cause GH release, including L-dopa and clonidine. In chapters three and four, you will gain some insight to the complexity and function of GH secretagogues.

The liver synthesizes insulin-like growth factors (IGF-I and II) as part of a feedback loop that regulates GH. The relationship between GH and IGF-I is extremely complex. Binding proteins and GH receptors are involved in how GH affects the body. African pygmies are a living example of the importance of GH receptors. One would think that giving pygmies GH would make them grow, but it doesn't. Pygmies have plenty of GH, but they are lacking receptor sites on their cells. Later, you will learn how to optimize IGF formation and sensitize GH and IGF-1 receptor sites in order to optimize response to GH therapy.

Treatment in the Early Days

From 1958 until the time it was finally synthesized, GH was painstakingly extracted from human cadavers and injected into GH-deficient children and adults. Heat was known to destroy this precious substance, so in the early days of GH treatment the extract could not be heated to the point of killing all contaminants. Consequently, some of the early GH batches, which came from people who harbored the catalyst for the human version of "mad cow" disease, were contaminated. Creutzfeldt-Jakob disease (CJD), as it is known, is a horribly debilitating brain disorder for which there is no known cure. CJD belongs to a family of diseases that afflict sheep, cows and humans. The prion that causes it is neither viral nor bacterial, but is thought to be a normal protein that has become distorted. Prion contamination ceased to be a problem when the FDA banned the natural version of GH and approved the synthesized version in 1985.

Synthetic GH Arrives

During the early 1980s, two phenomena occurred that would eventually lead to synthetic human GH; no longer would it have to be taken from cadavers. Yuppie fever hit, and DNA cloning was invented. Cloning allowed researchers, for the first time, to ferret out the individual sequences of DNA that code for proteins. The discovery of cloning techniques has fueled a scientific revolution that is still in its infancy. "Recombinant DNA" technology allows DNA to be snipped into little pieces with "molecular scissors" and placed into bacteria. The bacteria then churn out little Xerox copies of the snippet. By amplifying DNA in this fashion, it becomes possible to really study and understand individual sequences. This is how the DNA sequence that codes for GH was found. The first product of this method offered on a commercial scale was insulin. The second was GH. The same company, Genentech, synthesized both of them.

The large scale cloning of human GH had come about in large part because of the actions of congress, which, in 1983, wrote The Orphan Drug Act into law. The law was designed to provide incentive for drug companies to develop and market drugs that would help people with rare diseases. Many of these people were falling through the cracks because drug companies could not justify spending money to develop drugs for which there wasn't a large market. The law provided that the federal government would heavily subsidize the development of drugs that affected 200,000 or fewer people, and any drug company that took on the task would have a 7-year monopoly on the market.

Genentech wasted no time in applying for "Orphan" status for the development of GH. The "orphan" market for GH was 7,000 GH-deficient kids. These children have severely inhibited growth, a condition that doctors refer to as "hypopituitary dwarfism". By 1985, Protropin was FDA approved for hypopituitary dwarfism. Initial sales were estimated to be $4M. One might wonder. . . Why would the biotech darling of Wall Street go after a market comprised of only 7,000 children? GH, like insulin, has to be taken every day for life. With the monopoly provided by the Orphan Drug Act, there would be no competitive pricing. The company holding the monopoly on GH could name their price.

At $15,000 per child per year—the price Genentech decided on—the $4M market for GH quickly turned into an $150M market. By the third quarter of the first year Protropin was on the market, it raked in $23M. In 1987, Adelle Haley, financial analyst at Smith Barney, declared that "short stature is a small market". According to her, Protropin sales wouldn't go above $23.8M. Her financial soothsaying proved to be wrong. Protropin ended the year with $43.6M in sales. The following year, sales were at $86M, and by 1989 sales were $122M. In 1995 Genentech was predicting sales of $1B worldwide.

YUPPIES, Lawsuits, and the Government

Genentech got a big boost in sales by a social phenomenon. About the same time that Genentech hit the market with growth hormone, YUPPIE fever gripped America. The credo of YUPPIEdom was all the perfection money can buy. People with short kids soon found out that perfection could be bought for about $15,000 a year. The number of children diagnosed with hypopituitary dwarfism (the only condition for which GH was approved) rose to 15,000 in 1989, from the original 7,000 in 1985. By 1995, 30,000 children per year were diagnosed with it. Company spokesmen attributed the increase to enhanced diagnostic abilities on the part of pediatricians. The whole thing was out of control during the '80s. Jeremy Rifkin's anti-biotech group sued the National Institute of Health (NIH) to stop trials of GH on short kids, and the FDA and Congress launched an investigation of Genentech's promotion of the drug.

The pharmaceutical giant, Eli Lilly, wanted GH too. It successfully cloned GH a few months after Genentech, and called its version Humatrope. As far as Genentech was concerned, it was fine to clone Humatrope. It was not fine to put it on the market.

Despite Genentech's "orphan" protection, the FDA approved Humatrope in 1987. Genentech promptly sued the FDA. In September of 1987, the first of its claims were shot down in a federal court. This was not the end of the litigation, however. In all, five companies went after GH and each other. Both Hoffmann-LaRoche and Lilly ended up suing Genentech, and Genentech sued them back over patent rights. Lilly and Genentech wrangled in court for 8 years, with Lilly finally throwing in the towel, agreeing to pay Genentech at least $145M over several years.

Enormous Potential

Even as Genentech went to market with Protropin, the company knew it could be used for a lot more than just dwarfism. Before Genentech made the synthetic version, athletes—notably Olympic athletes—were injecting GH from cadavers. It was widely believed in the athletic community that GH could increase endurance and strength. This "underground" use of GH by athletes was problematic in two significant ways. First, pharmacological (as opposed to physiological) doses of GH were being used, secondly, the long term effects were unknown. A pharmacological dose is one that far exceeds levels that would occur naturally in the body. A pharmacological dose is designed to act like a drug on the body's systems. This is far different from the physiological doses being injected into kids to make them grow. A physiological dose merely brings levels up to normal. No one— including the athletes themselves—knew what the side effects of huge doses of GH would be. Because the natural hormone was undetectable, policing it was impossible.

Publicly, Genentech admitted that GH might be used for enhanced wound healing. Osteoporosis was a maybe. But the scientific literature contained tantalizing hints that the market for GH would be huge. Growth hormone affects many systems of the body; in fact, it targets nearly all tissues. The insulin-like effect of GH that results in lowering of blood glucose made it a very attractive target for diabetes research. In addition, GH was known to be "lipolytic" (fat burning). From the drug company's perspective, the fat-lowering, sugar-lowering capability of GH gave it an exciting and potentially huge market.

Hundreds of studies later, GH has become one of the most exciting hormones ever studied. The anti-aging potential is so great that the National Institute on Aging is conducting long-term, large-scale studies. There is nothing to suggest that GH won't live up to its reputation. Unlike other hormones with anti-aging potential, GH has been extensively studied in humans. The scientific literature is replete with new studies. GH has been associated with improvement in some of the most prevalent and intractable diseases of aging: Parkinson's disease, osteoporosis, heart disease and diabetes. And the good news is that people don't have to travel to Anterea to get it. It's available here—on earth.

"

I'm so excited about Symbiotropin. I have lost 30 inches in three months, it has burned the cellulite very fast off my legs and hips. The next best thing is my skin. My skin was so thin it was tearing almost daily… it is now thick again, it looks and feels like when I was much younger!! My age spots have disappeared from my hands… my eyes have improved so much I seldom wear my glasses anymore… I have increased my muscle mass and strength tremendously. My memory has really improved also. My hair is thicker and grows really, really fast…

– H.G. (Female, Age 57)

"

"After ninety, there's no need to worry about dying. Not many people die over the age of ninety."

– George Burns

CHAPTER TWO

MORE FACTS: CLINICAL STUDIES ON hGH

Recently, the FDA has approved hGH therapy for adults who are deficient, which includes nearly everyone over the age of 40. This is an important step in recognizing aging as a disease and opening the doors to the acceptance of a variety of anti-aging therapies. The approval of Humatrope, manufactured by Eli Lilly, is based on clinical data that demonstrate its effectiveness in increasing lean muscle mass, decreasing body fat, increasing exercise capacity, and raising HDL cholesterol ("good cholesterol") levels. Several major pharmaceutical companies have research teams who are racing to release the first FDA approved growth hormone secretagogue. There are already natural hGH secretagogues available over the counter, which are being continually refined and formulated to exceed the efficacy of growth hormone itself.

Why is there so much focus on growth hormone,

and what does all of this mean for those of us who suddenly have these substances available? To put it simply, there is no other substance known to man that has such far reaching ability to prevent and reverse the aging process.

Studies published in the New England Journal of Medicine and other journals show that hGH may reverse human biological aging by:

Restoring *muscle mass*
Decreasing *body fat*
Thickening the skin, *reducing wrinkles*
Restoring *lost hair*
Restoring *hair color*
Increasing *energy*
Increasing *sexual function*
Improving *cholesterol profile*
Restoring *size of liver, pancreas, heart and other organs that shrink with age*
Improving *vision*
Improving *memory*
Elevating *mood and improving sleep*
Normalizing *blood pressure*
Increasing *cardiac output and stamina*
Improving *immune function*
Assisting in *wound healing*

It may seem too good to be true that a single substance could have so many far-reaching effects, but as we look more closely at the scientific evidence from human studies and at the physiologic interaction between growth hormone and the body's various systems that affect these areas, everything begins to fall into place. By the time Dr. Rudman began his work in 1985, the safety of growth hormone had already been well established through its use in children with GH deficiency. Decades earlier, growth hormone from pituitary extract had been shown to decrease body fat significantly in laboratory rats. Dr. Rudman hypothesized that the changes in body composition which become apparent around age 35 had to do with declining hormone levels, and he began by testing hGH to examine its effects on lean body mass and body fat. Dr. Rudman studied 12 men between the ages of 61 and 80 who experienced significant changes in body composition with age, but who were otherwise healthy. These men were overweight and had significantly low levels of growth hormone. They were instructed not to alter their lifestyle in any way throughout the course of this six-month study. Despite the fact that they did not alter their diet, exercise, or smoking habits—the men who were given hGH gained an average of 8.8% in lean muscle mass while losing 14% of their body fat. They experienced localized increase in bone density and their skin became thicker and firmer. According to Rudman and his associates, the subjects of this study reversed these parameters of aging by 10-20 years. This represented the biggest breakthrough in anti-aging medicine at the time and led to a wide acceptance that, in the words of Dr. Rudman, "The overall deterioration of the body that comes with growing old is not inevitable."

In his study, Dr. Rudman used dosages of hGH that produced blood levels that exceeded those that the body would normally maintain. He and his researchers concluded that because these extremely high doses caused some side effects, including edema and carpal tunnel syndrome, "the optimum hormone dose is only one quarter to one half as great as was previously believed."

Subsequent studies have confirmed the conclusions of Dr. Rudman's study to show that lower doses of growth hormone used to replace diminished levels within a physiologic boundary, produce the same degree of benefit without any side effects. Studies done in Europe and in the United States demonstrate that hGH therapy, when used properly, improves cardiac output and stamina while restoring many of the other functions to potentially extend length and quality of life.

Metabolic Rate

In 1989, Dr. Franco Salomon and his associates in London, England demonstrated that growth hormone given to deficient adults over a course of 6 months resulted in an increase in lean body mass of over 10% and a 7% reduction of body fat. These subjects experienced an increase in basal metabolic rate as well as improved strength and exercise performance, which had previously been below normal.

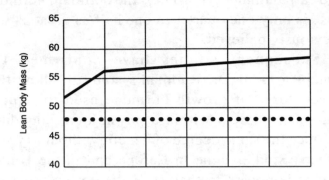

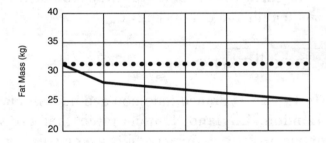

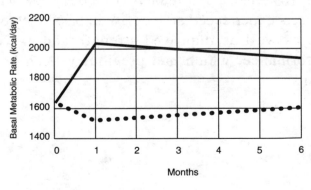

Months

——————— Recombinant Human Growth Hormone

• • • • • • Placebo

Heart Failure

In Italy, Dr. Serafino Fazio et al recently evaluated the effects of growth hormone with moderate to severe heart failure. The researchers found that hGH, when combined with standard heart failure treatment, resulted in increased efficiency of the heart's energy consumption and ability to pump a higher volume of blood while increasing circulation by reducing peripheral vascular resistance. This research opens the door for growth hormone to not only enhance cardiovascular output in healthy people, but to be used as an adjunctive treatment for patients with heart disease.

Osteoporosis

Adults who are growth hormone deficient are known to have low bone density. Growth hormone has a significant effect on the formation of new bone tissue and, as we will see in the work that Dr. Chein has done, seems to have a significant effect on restoring lost bone tissue. Standard medical protocols offer the option of slowing bone loss, but they do not cause new bone to be formed. GH and IGF-1 both stimulate osteoblast activity, which increases the formation of new bone. With standard therapy as it exists, most medical doctors would not expect to see any measurable increase in bone density in one year, yet increases of 3% to 5% per year are standard for many patients receiving growth hormone therapy.

Wasting Diseases

Growth Hormone is known to increase the uptake of amino acids by muscle cells, making it an excellent candidate for patients with wasting diseases like AIDS. People who experience high levels of physiologic stress such as surgery or severe burns often have difficulty in recovery from injury and develop symptoms of wasting. The use of growth hormone in these circumstances has been successful and continued study is underway. One of the underlying problems in recovering from muscle wasting is the inability to properly absorb nutrients; growth hormone not only assists in muscle formation, but in the absorption of nutrients in the digestive tract.

Digestive Tract Disorders

Studies by Doug Wilmore, M.D. and associates at Harvard's Brigham & Women's Hospital in Boston demonstrate the effectiveness of hGH injections combined with the amino acid L-Glutamine in regenerating the digestive tracts of patients with short bowel syndrome. Before therapy, the digestive tracts of these patients were incapable of digesting food; hence, patients had to be fed intravenously. After therapy, the same patients were able to eat solid food and absorb nutrients effectively. This work holds great promise for the number of people with colitis and Crohn's disease whose diseases typically continue to worsen with standard medical protocols. It also suggests yet another way that growth hormone therapy works to reverse the aging process. All of us experience a decline in nutrient absorption as we age due to the thinning of the lining of the digestive tract. In fact, the permeability of the digestive tract lining has been directly correlated with the onset of a variety of illnesses. When the digestive tract lining becomes very thin a patient may be told that she has Leaky Gut Syndrome—a condition that may lead to a variety of autoimmune diseases, rheumatism, allergies, and arthritis.

202 Patients

The largest study of the effects of growth hormone on humans has taken place at the Palm Springs Life Extension Institute under the direction of Dr. Edmund Chein, director of the institute, and his associate Dr. Leon Terry, a neuroendocrinologist from the Department of Neurology at the Medical College of Wisconsin. Dr. Chein follows a growth hormone protocol that involves restoring GH levels for patients who are deficient (IGF-1 less than 350 ng/ml) with low dose, high frequency injections. Dr. Chein, by combining hGH with other hormones that are shown to be low, has developed a program that he claims has been 100% effective for all of his patients. He guarantees that his patients will experience an increase in bone density of 1.5 - 2.5% every 6 months, as well as a loss of 10% body fat and an increase of 10% muscle mass. These processes may continue until the patient attains the body composition of a twenty-year-old.

Recently, Dr. Terry collected the data of patients

who have been treated at the Life Extension Institute and has written up the amazing results. The following assessment figures were derived from 308 randomly selected self-assessment questionnaires that were completed by 202 patients during the term of their therapy between the years of 1994 and 1996.

ASSESSMENT
Effects of Growth Hormone Administration
(Low Dose-High Frequency)
in 202 Patients
L. Cass Terry, M.D., Ph.D. & Edmund Chein, M.D.
Medical College of Wisconsin
& Palm Springs Life Extension Institute

IMPROVEMENT

Strength, Exercise & Body Fat

Muscle Strength 88%

Muscle Size 81%

Body Fat Loss 72%

Exercise Tolerance 81%

Exercise Endurance 83%

Skin & Hair

Skin Texture 71%

Skin Thickness 68%

Skin Elasticity 71%

Wrinkle Disappearance 51%

New Hair Growth 38%

Healing, Flexibility & Resistance

Healing of old injuries 55%

Healing of other injuries 61%

Healing Capacity 71%

Back Flexibility 53%

Resistance to Common Illness 73%

Sexual Function

Sexual Potency/Frequency 75%

Duration of Penile Erection 62%

Frequency of Nighttime Urination 57%

Hot Flashes 58%

Menstrual Cycle Regulation 39%

Energy, Emotions, & Memory

Energy Level 84%

Emotional Stability 67%

Attitude Toward Life 78%

Memory 62%

In general, these improvements were reported to occur within 1 to 3 months of the onset of therapy with a tendency to continue improving over 6 months of treatment. Chein and Terry are currently studying the effects of hGH replacement therapy on triglycerides, HDL and LDL cholesterol, PSA, blood pressure, and cardiovascular fitness.

It is important to note that Drs. Chein and Terry believe in a total approach to deterring the aging process by replacing a variety of hormones that are deficient, using aerobic and resistance training, dietary evaluation, and stress reduction. We believe in the importance of this well-rounded approach as well. From clinical experience, when a wider range of hormones are replaced to overcome deficiency, greater results may be obtained with lower doses. As we detail in future chapters, using the proper diet and exercise techniques to stabilize insulin and enhance growth hormone release are essential to attaining optimal results.

Chein and Terry have demonstrated a 61% increase in IGF-1 levels after 1 to 2 months of hGH therapy with low dose high frequency (LD-HF) injections without the major side effects found in studies that involve much higher dose lower frequency injection of hGH. However, some patients experienced minor joint pain and fluid retention, which disappeared after the initial two months of therapy. While the LD-HF protocol appears to more closely mimic the patterns of the body's own growth hormone release when compared with the high dose low frequency dosing used by Rudman; it does not precisely duplicate our natural release patterns. This may account for the minor side effects found in Chein's patients.

Can the Side Effects be Overcome?

Upon recognizing the importance of restoring growth hormone to physiologic levels in order to maximize the effectiveness and reduce side effects, it is important to examine the effects of natural secretagogues. Natural secretagogues may be our best hope for raising growth hormone in an entirely physiologic manner because of the ability to stimulate the endocrine system to release its own growth hormone. Reference to the stimulation of the endocrine system rather than the pituitary alone, reflects the complex interactions among the liver, pancreas, adrenals, thyroid, hypothalamus, and pituitary that effect the release and response to growth hormone.

> *"Once we've identified the right materials to use, the most challenging obstacles in attaining consistent and significant growth hormone release are 1) absorption and 2) delivery to the proper receptor sites. Our team has researched and developed an array of Chaperone Molecule delivery systems that address gastric absorption, transport through the bloodstream, and attachment to appropriate receptors. What's exciting is that we're using all natural substances."*
>
> – Pharmacologist James Jamieson

There are a variety of nutrients and other natural substances that have been demonstrated to increase the release of growth hormone. For instance, the amino acid L-glutamine has been shown to increase growth hormone by 15%, while the endogenously produced substance, L-dopa, has been shown to restore youthful levels of growth hormone for men over the age of 60. The amino acid arginine is used as a standard in measuring growth hormone secretory potential, where the patient is loaded with arginine and subsequent IGF-1 levels are measured. It is plausible that the proper combination of natural substances could produce a synergistic effect that would exceed that of any single nutrient if the proper knowledge of biochemistry and clinical response were combined with the right pharmacology. But, in order to arrive at an effective means of accomplishing this – we must understand...

"―――――――――――――――――――――

I've noticed my hair is turning darker.

– M.B. (Female, Age 76)

"I saw a definite change in my overall feeling within a few weeks. I am 62 years old and before starting this regime, I felt like I was 82. After 2 months I now breathe better with no more wheezing, my body is firmer, my stamina has improved, my memory is much better and I feel as if I were a 45 year old again."

– B.S. (Male, Age 62)

―――――――――――――――――――――**"**

*"Attention to health is life's
greatest hindrance."*

– Plato

"Plato was a bore."

– Nietzsche

CHAPTER THREE

THE NATURE OF hGH SECRETAGOGUES

Secretagogue: that which stimulates secreting organs. Many substances stimulate the release of growth hormone from the pituitary gland. Amino acids, drugs, and exercise are among the provocateurs. Despite the phenomenal success of synthetic GH, scientists are in hot pursuit of factors that can be taken orally to stimulate the pituitary to release GH. Recombinant GH is problematic: it has to be injected—in most cases several times a day. It is expensive—way outside the budget of many people who would otherwise benefit. It has side effects and probably downregulates receptors, which means that its effects diminish over time. Researchers realize that what is needed is something that can be taken orally to stimulate the natural secretion of GH. This must be accomplished in a way that will prevent over stimulation to the point of downregulation, but at the same time increase the hormone to a level that will elicit a response. Some of the important advantages to GH secretagogues include preservation of feedback mechanisms that modulate GH response and generation of pulsatile patterns of GH release, which more closely mimic natural secretion.

Possible Side Effects
Associated with GH Injections
- Cancer
- Hypotension
- Congestive Heart Disease
- Uncontrolled Bleeding
- Carpal Tunnel Syndrome
- Reduced Insulin Sensitivity
- Hypoglycemia
- Hyperglycemia
- G.I. Disturbances
- Gynecomastia
- Edema
- Leukemia in Children
- Ketogenesis
- Allergic Response

The Evolution of Secretagogue Research

Synthesis of GH in the '80s. led to an explosion of GH research. The list of potential beneficiaries grew to include AIDS patients, burn victims, patients with Turner's syndrome, those receiving glucocorticoids and chemotherapy, and of course the elderly.

While some researchers pursued the effects of injected synthetic GH, others focused on finding GH secretagogues. In 1977, Dr. Roger Guillemin was awarded the Nobel Prize for his work on GH. Guillemin discovered the two hormones that are known to control GH. Both originate in the hypothalamus. One is called growth hormone releasing hormone (GHRH) and the other is somatostatin. GHRH stimulates growth hormone release, while somatostatin inhibits it. The discovery of these hormones marked the recognition of auxiliary substances that would affect GH status, and initiated a search for the perfect secretagogue.

The Morphine Connection

Frank Momany, Cyril Bowers and their group discovered the first synthetic secretagogue. It was called growth hormone releasing peptide 6 (GHRP-6) in reference to its six constituent amino acids. Strangely enough, the discovery of GHRP-6 came from research on morphine addiction.

In the 1920s, it was noted that female morphine addicts were often sterile. A few curious scientists tried to study the phenomenon by recreating the situation in rats. But no matter how much morphine they injected, sterility could not be induced. In 1934, a researcher named Ko tried it in mice and it worked. Three years later another researcher, Bun, did the same in rabbits with the same result. But because the model couldn't be recreated in rats, researchers shied away from studying it further.

In 1949, Dr. Charles Barraclough and his colleague Everett discovered that the hormone that induces the reproductive cycle is released only at a certain time of the day. Previous researchers had been injecting rats at the wrong time! Barraclough and another colleague, Sawyer, quickly demonstrated that if given at the right time of the day, morphine blocked the reproductive cycle in rats. At that time, they theorized that the signal that caused the pituitary to release the reproductive hormone originated in the hypothalamus. While it didn't seem very important at the time, the knowledge that morphine affected a pituitary hormone eventually became very important.

In 1972, Dr. Paul Cushman was looking to define more specifically the effect that morphine has on the pituitary. At that time, GH was considered the "most sensitive index of pituitary function". So Cushman set up studies to measure GH in morphine addicts. Unfortunately, because of problems in methodology and the small number of people studied, he could draw no sound conclusions about the effects of morphine on the pituitary or GH. But the first inkling that GH is under control of an opioid was had. The following year, researchers at the University of California, Irvine demonstrated conclusively that morphine increases GH.

Three years later, it was shown that morphine initially increases GH levels, then causes them to decline. That same year, researchers found "natural" morphine in the body, and the pieces of the puzzle started coming together. Did natural morphine, like synthetic morphine, increase GH? Later that year, Dr. John Hughes and his group synthesized natural morphine. It turned out to be two pentapeptides (5 amino acids). They called the substance "enkephalin". Enkephalin caused the release of GH. It was a natural secretagogue. For the next 5 years, dozens of researchers shuffled the amino acid sequence of enkephalin, hoping to find a GH secretagogue they could patent. Many analogues of enkephalin were reported to increase GH, but nothing was pursued for commercial use. Gradually, most researchers abandoned the hunt for the perfect peptide.

Momany and Bowers of Tulane University continued refining their sequences until finally, in 1979, they came up with a peptide that was active orally. The hexapeptide (6 amino acids) was known as "growth hormone releasing peptide-6" (GHRP-6). The peptide is: His-DTrp-Ala-Trp-DPhe-Lys-NH2. Although GHRP-6 was active when taken orally, it didn't cause enough GH enhancement to be patented and sold as a drug. Momany, Bowers and others have used GHRP-6 as a launching pad to create other, more potent secretagogues. One of them, Hexarelin, is currently undergoing trials. Momany continues to study potential secretagogues for GH and other hormones, using sophisticated computer modeling to combine and recombine the amino acids.

You may note the "D" prefix to some of the amino acids in the GHRP-6 sequence. This is common to all major secretagogue peptides that have been studied. The natural form of these constituent amino acids is the "L" form, but for proprietary and stability reasons—they have been replaced with the synthetic "D" form. This is not the case with the naturally derived peptide secretagogues that we will describe later.

GHRP-6 and its derivatives are peptide secretagogues, but non-peptide secretagogues have been created. Using molecular modeling, researchers at Merck have designed a drug (presently known as MK677) that mimics the effect of GHRP-6. It works by artificially inducing similar kinds of changes in cell membranes caused by GHRP-6. Its chemical structure is similar to benzodiazepine drugs.

It is interesting to note that, like growth hormone injections, none of the synthesized secretagogues address the systemic influences of GH such as IGF-1 formation and receptor sites. This probably explains the mixed results that they have produced in terms of consistent IGF-1 stimulation and the lack of symptomatic improvement, which have impeded their success.

In this assessment, we cannot ignore the natural GH secretagogues that originate within the body (endogenous) and outside the body (exogenous). Estrogen and testosterone enhance GH, as do the amino acids arginine and ornithine. The vitamin niacin (B3, niacinamide) enhances GH by reducing free fatty acids. Fasting enhances GH, and so does intense, sustained exercise. However, none of these by themselves increase GH enough, or in the proper way, to be considered a true GH enhancement therapy. But, as you are about to discover, the proper combination of peptides, pharmaceutical sugars, amino acids, diet, and exercise can produce significant and measurable age reversing effects. And it's a lot simpler than it sounds.

Intrinsic Factors that Affect GH Release

There are several factors that control GH release in a manner that may limit response to secretagogue therapies. We have reviewed the hypothalamic hormones, GHRH and somatostatin, and their direct role in regulating GH secretion, but GH regulation is far more complex. In addition to pituitary receptors for which corresponding hormones have not yet been identified, there are direct influences that come from each of the minerals potassium, magnesium, calcium, and zinc. The dominant memory neurotransmitter, acetyl-choline, regulates GH secretion, while blood pH and feedback mechanisms from IGF-1 and IGF-2 play important roles. Other factors, such as hGH binding proteins and metabolic clearance rate directly limit symptomatic response to growth hormone.

These are only some of the intrinsic factors that have been identified, and upon examining them, we begin to gain an appreciation for the years of research that have been performed on hGH secretagogues and the complexity involved in a substance that works not only to elicit GH release, but consistent symptomatic response.

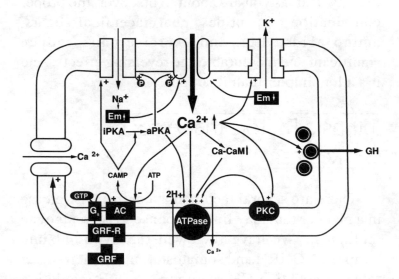

Model depicting the pathways responsible for the
GHRH – induced increase in [Ca++], and GH release in somatotrophs.

This graphic representation illustrates some of the known mechanisms by which calcium (Ca++) elicits the release of GH from pituitary somatotrophs. Ca++ increase is associated with an increase in GHRH.

Interestingly, any rise in Ca++, independent of GHRH, will cause the release of GH, and any fall in Ca++ will cause a diminished release of GH. The pulsatile secretion pattern of growth hormone has been directly associated with rhythmic rises in Ca++. One of the mechanisms by which somatostatin works to block GH secretion is through inhibition of Ca++ and potentiation of potassium (K+).

Zinc deficiency is known to profoundly affect the GH/IGF-1 axis. Many of the signs of zinc deficiency are directly associated with the action of growth hormone, including poor wound healing, reduced protein synthesis, immunosuppression, and reduced sex hormone concentrations. Zinc, magnesium, and potassium deficiencies can all negatively affect circulating IGF-1.

In addition to the intricacies involved in its release, there is a great degree of complexity associated with the growth hormone molecule itself. Although most attention in focused on 22-kd hGH, "free GH", which accounts for only 20% of the over 100 naturally occurring forms of hGH that have been identified, the role of the other 80% of various forms of hGH is not yet fully understood. Research shows that GH bound to growth hormone with GH binding protein ($hGH(hGHbp)_2$) plays an important role in maintaining and enhancing the activity of growth hormone. Interestingly, the $hGH(hGHbp)_2$ molecule is structurally identical to the free form of porcine growth hormone—the form that is predominant in the porcine pituitary, a primary ingredient in Symbiotropin.

Some of the details, which we have merely brushed the surface of here, begin to give us a flavor for the complexity of an effective GH secretagogue. Individual amino acids, vitamins, peptides and prescription drugs may bring about some type of GH release, but without creating the proper environment, results are limited.

"

I do not have to get up to urinate at night as frequently.

– O.B. (Male, Age 76)

I had severe emphysema, and it has improved greatly.

-F.B. (Male, Age 67)

"

*"Each problem that I solved became a
rule, which served afterwards to
solve other problems."*

– Rene Descartes, "Discours de la Methode"

CHAPTER FOUR

IN PURSUIT OF THE METHUSELAH FACTOR

BY PHARMACOLOGIST JAMES JAMIESON

*"A substance that has the action of a hormone, but
has not been purified & identified as a distinct
chemical compound is called a factor."*

As we have reviewed in chapter one, there has
been an evolution of hGH from its original source
as a glandular tissue extract to its existence today as
a product of recombinant DNA synthesis. Paralleling
this evolution, are pharmaceutical innovations that
allow the manipulation of microbes to produce
therapeutic proteins and the discovery of previously
unrecognized receptors that affect GH release and
conversion to IGF-1. Long before these discoveries,
there were medicinal plants that we can now process
and grow to be highly effective promoters of growth
hormone secretion. The story of the development of
Symbiotropin, a natural secretagogue compound, is
influenced by all of these aspects of pharmaceutical

technology and begins with my work in developing prescription hormone products in the 60's and 70's.

> *Genetic engineering has been a catalyst in the discovery of therapeutic proteins to replace deficient, missing or damaged hormones.*

As a third generation pharmacologist, my family had already established a reputation for producing effective hormone products from glandular and other sources. So it came as no surprise when I was approached by physicians and pharmaceutical companies in the early 70's to provide them with Human Chorionic Gonadotrophin (HCG). At the time, HCG was being used as a treatment for obesity, and although it was not approved for this application, it had become rapidly popularized because of its profound ability to cause significant weight loss very quickly. While overweight patients were losing 30 or more pounds per month without side effects, word spread and the demand for HCG began to exceed the supply.

Like growth hormone, HCG was not convenient to use because it had to be injected, hence the cost was high and compliance was limited. No one had challenged the delivery of HCG as an injection because it was known to be broken down and rendered ineffective when administered orally. As a person who enjoys attempting to do the impossible, I set forth the challenge to produce the first effective HCG in an oral dosage form. I had to figure out a way to protect and stabilize this molecule throughout its entire route from the capsule, across the digestive tract, into the bloodstream, and finally to the targeted receptors. After researching the transport mechanisms of HCG, I began to experiment with various complimentary molecules that would serve to protect against hydrochloric acid and other destructive influences. I eventually found the right substances to combine with HCG and created the first oral dosage form of this hormone.

GH is a Very Large Molecule, Which Is Unstable, Expensive and Difficult to Manufacture

GH, or somatotropic hormone (SH) is a small protein molecule containing 191 amino acids in a single chain with a total molecular weight of 22,005. Other posterior pituitary hormones, such as antidiuretic hormone (ADH), vasopressin, and oxytocin, are polypeptides containing nine amino acids.

My work with HCG led to the discovery of over 300 molecules, now referred to as *chaperone molecules*, that I have used to facilitate delivery of hormones and other sensitive compounds. Most producers of pharmaceutical hormones use the attachment of chemical side chains to transcend absorption problems, often resulting in unwanted side effects. On the other hand, the use of natural chaperone molecules allows hormones from plants and tissue extracts to be absorbed and utilized in their natural state.

Eli Lilly is spending $60 million for research on technology that we already have!

Eli Lilly to Help Fund Emisphere's Work On Oral Drug Delivery

By a WALL STREET JOURNAL Staff Reporter

INDIANAPOLIS–Eli Lilly & Co. agreed to help fund Emisphere Technologies Inc.'s development of "carrier molecules" that would allow oral delivery of Lilly drugs that currently must be injected.

The research alliance could provide Emisphere, a Hawthorne, N.Y., biopharmaceutical concern, with as much as $60 million in initial fees, research funding, and subsequent "milestone" and other payments.

The major focus of the collaboration, the ˇpanies said, will be in "the area of ˇrinology, including growth disorders." ˇˇˇ growth hormone, used in treating ˇˇˇˇˇ ˇˇˇˇˇ ˇˇˇˇˇˇ

Chaperone molecules assist in digestive tract absorption as well as delivery to the proper receptors. Hence, it is necessary to define the receptors that the active ingredients are targeting. All of the major anterior pituitary hormones, except growth hormone, exert their primary effect by stimulating target glands. GH exerts its effect on almost all tissues of the body. This presents a significant challenge in going beyond GH stimulation to elicit a response to GH and IGF-1 at the tissue level. With the aging process, we not only experience reduced production of growth hormone, but desensitization of receptors. One factor that affects this desensitization is the blockage of these receptor sites by environmental toxins and other substances. These receptors must be unblocked in order to benefit fully from growth hormone therapy. This "unblocking" process takes place under the influence of polysaccharide chaperones molecules and specific plant compounds, which I describe as Pharmafoods.

The body often has alternative pathways of hormonal activity that are responsive to natural plant-based substances, or Pharmafoods—several of which are incorporated in Symbiotropin. These natural compounds, which are on their way to becoming the medicines of the 21st century, assist the body in healing itself in spite of mistreatment with various hormone-mimicking chemicals that are now part of our environment. Pharmafoods help to displace these unwanted chemicals and clear the way for effective hormone replacement.

> *The pharmacologic effects of plant-derived compounds are well-documented in both human and animal clinical trials. Some of the mechanisms of action are still being elucidated. Two definite pathways for the biological actions involve binding to hormone receptor sites or to enzymes that metabolize hormones; specifically, binding to steroid and prostaglandin dehydrogenase enzymes. Structural similarities between various plant compounds and their counterparts that are produced by the body enhance this affinity.*

Over the decades, I have continually used glandular extracts because they provide therapeutic hormones in a natural form that the body can recognize, respond to, and properly metabolize. Glandulars are not only used as a hormone source, but as a support for similar tissues in our own bodies. Research has shown that ingesting a tissue substance will attenuate autoimmune responses to counterpart tissues in the body. European doctors have many applications for glandular therapies, including immune stimulation with thymus extract and reduction of inflammation with pancreatic extracts. The emphasis on glandulars in European medicine led me to study and train there in the areas of cryotechnology, ultrafiltrations, xenogenic cell and tissue suspension, lyophilisates, and other methods of glandular tissue preparation. My studies in Europe eventually led me to Hungary where I had the honor of working with the brilliant scientist Tibor Kopjas, M.D.. Dr. Kopjas and I became deeply involved in studying pancreatic extracts for their anti-inflammatory and anti-tumor activities as well as their effect on hormone production and modulation.

My work in Europe led to an appreciation for the quality standards and techniques involved in glandular therapies, which is not found in the United States. European glandular products come from animals that are bred solely for this medicinal purpose under highly regulated conditions that control grazing, hygiene, feeding, breeding, and slaughtering. These animals are recognized for their pharmaceutical purpose, hence they are raised in a pharmaceutically controlled environment and carefully processed to yield appropriate results.

Symbiotropin incorporates the use of anterior pituitary peptides that have known effects on GH release. Through advanced processing, the activity of these peptides is maintained at a level that exceeds most live cell pituitary extracts. Originally, GHRH was the only known growth hormone releaser for which pituitary receptors had been identified, it was thought that other releasers worked indirectly on the pituitary. Since then, other GH releasing peptide receptors, which still remain nameless, have been discovered on the pituitary—indicating that there are other GH releasing hormones that have not been discovered or named. Some of these peptides are currently under investigation by pharmaceutical researchers, but they are usually injected because of the tendency of fragile proteins to be broken down in the digestive tract. If they only knew about Chaperone Molecules...

> *Growth hormone secretion is controlled by two hypothalamic peptides: growth hormone releasing hormone (GHRH), which stimulates it, and somatostatin, which inhibits it. Current bioengineered secretagogues ignore these basic principals.*

In working with hormone therapies in the early seventies, I developed a prescription product called Aphrodex that was used to promote sex drive in men. We yielded a much greater overall benefit by combining testosterone with the herb yohimbe and the homeopathic nux vomica, than we could by using any of the ingredients separately, hence we were able to use a lower dose of testosterone, which may cause side effects when used in excess. As a supplier of raw materials, I had been synthesizing DHEA and other hormones from wild yams and I became intrigued by the similarity of diosgenin in these yams to various adrenal hormones. But after observing the powerful synergy of the hormonally active botanical product and the isolated hormone in Aphrodex, I was inspired to study and identify hundreds of previously unrecognized botanical compounds that support and mimic the body's own hormones.

The study of plants and the therapeutic hormonal substances contained in them led to a clearer understanding of hormone receptors in the body and techniques for overcoming those that have become blocked. I also observed the importance of processing these plants in a way that would allow me to derive a standardized amount of a given substance without the use of chemicals and without denaturing the enzymes and other components of the plant. As much as I was discovering all of these "new" individual active compounds, I also discovered the importance of preserving the activity of all of the plant's components—so as not to second-guess nature. This is not always an easy task; in fact, it takes a lot more time and money than the methods that are used by most processors of herbs today.

Each plant has its own characteristics that must be taken into account in processing and standardizing its active ingredients. Most raw material suppliers of standardized herbs use a variety of chemicals, such as methyl chloride, that denature some components of the original plant and are left in significant amounts in the end product. The people who consume these herbs often have no idea that they are ingesting various toxic chemicals along with them. This doesn't work for me. Not only do natural processes of concentrating botanicals, like fermentation, allow the avoidance of chemicals, but they also preserve active enzymes and allow the full therapeutic potential of the whole plant to be realized.

In the development of Symbiotropin, I was led to the rain forest where I had done extensive work with botanicals in the past and had established valuable business connections. I discovered that a major pharmaceutical company was using a local botanical product in the development of a prescription secretagogue. This is not unusual as a large portion of prescription drugs are derived from plant sources by first isolating one active ingredient, denaturing it with a chemical side chain in order to patent it, then performing extensive clinical studies and finally submitting it, 21 million dollars later, to the FDA for approval. Upon examination, I found that the "active" ingredient was enhanced by the plant's other components. Further, we found that a large amount of the activity of this ingredient was lost very rapidly (within 2 hours) after harvesting. One of the active ingredients in this plant is L-dopa, a potent stimulator of GH release. I had worked extensively with L-dopa in the past as a consultant on its delivery. L-dopa, used as an anti-aging drug and treatment for Parkinson's disease, is poorly absorbed and must be taken in super-physiologic doses (thousands of times what the body would produce in a day) in order to elicit a response. At high doses, L-dopa can produce side effects, but at lower doses it will stimulate GH release, improve mental performance, and improve symptoms of Parkinson's disease. As was the case in all of my experience with other botanicals, the auxiliary substances in vicia faba major enhanced the activity and absorption of its naturally occurring L-dopa so that it would become a highly active secretagogue at lower doses and without the side effects of prescription L-dopa.

The effectiveness of Symbiotropin in Parkinson's patients has not been established through double blind clinical trials. However, there have been reports of rapid improvement in tremors and overall sense of well being. Growth hormone itself has produced improvements in Parkinson's disease; with the dual action of L-dopa and other secretagogues in Symbiotropin, and the lack of side effects, it's definitely worth a try for physician's to observe its affect on patients who suffer from this devastating disease.

Studies conducted on the effectiveness of various amino acid stimulants of growth hormone release have produced significant results. One test for GH secretory potential is the arginine loading test, but very large amounts are used—often intravenously. Other amino acids like ornithine, lysine, and glutamine have produced mixed results. In the development of Symbiotropin, I had to ask myself, "How could the response to these amino acids vary to such a large extent?"

As it turns out, the study on L-glutamine that produced the most significant elevation in GH administered the amino acid in a carbonated drink solution. How could carbonation make that much of a difference in the effectiveness of this amino acid in GH release? I had tested effervescent delivery with L-dopa and other substances in the past and found it to be highly effective in combination with Chaperone Molecules. With carbonation, I had been able to produce rapid and efficient delivery of sensitive compounds. In this case, I discovered that effervescent delivery assists in the delivery of all amino acids in Symbiotropin so that a greater and more consistent response can be derived with lower doses.

There are many receptors for these amino acids,

so getting them to the right ones that stimulate GH release requires the use of Chaperone Molecules. In addition to protecting and delivering these amino acids, some Chaperone Molecules have insulin-regulating effects.

The importance of suppressing insulin in provoking GH release cannot be overstated. Blood sugar and insulin inhibit the release of growth hormone—this is a basic principle of the effectiveness of proper diet, fasting and exercise in stimulating GH. While consuming sugar and other carbohydrates in the diet will provoke insulin and inhibit GH release, there are other sugars, referred to as pharmaceutical saccharides that do not provoke insulin and are not metabolized as carbohydrates. In fact, when the right saccharides are used they do just the opposite—they help to regulate blood sugar and insulin. Some of these saccharides—like those in Symbiotropin—have a sweet taste, which eliminates the need for artificial or high carbohydrate sweeteners in flavoring the product.

I am not implying that insulin is the bad guy. In this highly complex system, we need insulin to promote the benefits of growth hormone. Studies show that GH fails to cause growth in animals lacking a pancreas and it also fails if carbohydrates (insulin provoking) are restricted from the diet. These studies reinforce our knowledge of insulin as a necessary catalyst in GH response and demonstrate that high levels of GH mean nothing in terms of results. This is why I have concentrated on secretagogues, receptor site modulators, insulin regulation, and liver enzyme enhancers rather than GH injections.

> *As adequate availability of specific complex sugars, which only work in conjunction with insulin, is necessary for GH to be effective—it is interesting to note that bioengineered GH injectables significantly lower insulin levels—what will the long term effects be?*

Upon examining the influences on GH and IGF-1, and looking further at their complex interaction with other hormones that are centrally controlled by the pituitary gland, it becomes apparent that the Methuselah factor is contained within the pituitary system. There are many ways in which we interfere with the proper functioning of this gland and other endocrine organs— including improper diet and exposure to environmental toxins that block receptors with their hormone-mimicking effects. At the same time, we have the tools to optimize the dietary influence on endocrine function and to unblock clogged receptors with the use of natural compounds. When we supply the proper peptides and other compounds, we "kick-start" optimal pituitary function, but we must not ignore pituitary feedback mechanisms that are affected by other hormones and the synergy that occurs when all hormones are addressed. It is a highly complex system, but as we develop a full understanding of the elusive Methuselah factor and its role in the maintenance of other hormones, perhaps we are creating the choice to live for hundreds of years.

There are over 110,000 genes in the human body—one million partial gene sequences have been identified. A new paradigm of pharmaceutical innovation is focusing on new hormones and microbial genes to broaden and accelerate the discovery of small molecule drugs. These new types of medicines include gene therapy, protein therapy, and anti-sense therapies. This method of small molecule drug discovery analyzes genes expressed only in diseased or target tissues and is catalyzing the change from current interdiction based medicine to gene based prevention.

With this research, we have gained access to therapeutic proteins that replace deficient, missing, or damaged hormones. Some of these synthesized peptides are currently under investigation as growth hormone secretagogues, but their naturally occurring counterparts are contained in Symbiotropin—an all natural GH secretagogue. Once we've identified the right peptides to use, the most challenging obstacles in attaining consistent and significant growth hormone release are absorption and delivery to the proper receptor sites. Our team has researched and developed an array of Chaperone Molecule delivery systems that address gastric absorption, transport through the bloodstream, and attachment to appropriate receptors.

Research on various synthesized peptide secretagogues has produced limited results in terms of IGF-1 formation and symptomatic improvement because they do not address insulin regulation, hepatic formation of IGF-1, or IGF-1 receptors. The pharmacologic effects of plant derived compounds are well documented in both human and animal clinical trials. These plant products possess structural similarities to endogenously produced hormones, which enhance their affinity to hormone receptors and steroid and prostaglandin dehydrogenases—making them effective adjuncts to a variety of hormone replacement therapies.

As we more fully understand the decline of endocrine function in the aging patient, we are recognizing the benefits of replacing a wider range of hormones—where lower doses produce a greater overall benefit. Central to HRT response is management of growth hormone, insulin, and IGF-1. These hormones potentiate the function of estrogen, testosterone, progesterone, T3, and other hormones. Unlike these other hormones, which decline in production with age, growth hormone continues to be produced in significant amounts right into old age. The challenge in restoring youthful levels of GH is not increasing production or injecting the hormone itself, but releasing it from its sequestered state. We now know how to unlock the gates that keep GH from circulating.

Studies on GH injections repeatedly demonstrate its effectiveness at reversing signs of aging by improving body composition, increasing bone density, reducing wrinkles, restoring hair, improving cardiac output, reducing cholesterol, and improving vision and memory. In addition, our clinical observations with Symbiotropin have yielded swift and significant improvement in diabetes and high blood pressure—even in patients whose symptoms were not able to be controlled with standard treatments. Insulin and IGF-1 regulation is an integral part of managing many of the signs and symptoms of aging.

A MESSAGE TO DOCTORS

As the FDA has recently approved growth hormone therapy for adults who are deficient, which includes most people over the age of 40, we are coming closer to the treatment of aging as a disease. In the replacement of deficient hormones, it is incumbent upon us to use the safest and most effective forms of these hormones. We are not limited to synthetic hormones that the body does not recognize and metabolize as its own, and which are associated with serious side effects. There are natural, safe, and effective forms of estrogen, progesterone, testosterone, thyroid hormone, DHEA, and other hormones that are identical to our own hormones. These hormones are available in dosage forms that maximize bioavailability and maintain effectiveness at physiologic doses. If our goal is to replace missing hormones, why shouldn't we replace them naturally? What could be more natural than utilizing the growth hormone that continues to be produced by our own pituitary?

James Jamieson

"The Cancer Center (1-800-720-8933; cancernet.com) has had first hand confirmatory experience that Lissoni's reports from Italy asserting efficacy for cancer treatment of combined interleukin-2 (IL-2) and melatonin for many forms of adult cancer are valid. We believe immunotherapy has now advanced to the degree that it is a lifesaving, albeit less well studied, alternative to conventional cytotoxic chemotherapy for many patients, including those with adenocarcinoma of colon, pancreatic, breast, or lung origin. Once natural killer (NK) lymphocytes have reached two or three times the normal level, we have found [Symbiotropin] very useful to reduce the malaise often associated with high blood levels of NK cells. We have instances where the addition of [Symbiotropin] to (IL-2) therapy allowed us to restore debilitated previous recipients of combination chemotherapy and allowed continued use of (IL-2) and was associated with continued shrinkage of the cancer as evidenced by successive drops in serologic markers such as CEA or BR27.29."

R. Arnold Smith, Jr., M.D.
S. North Central Mississippi Regional Cancer Center

J.M., Female, Age 71

Began taking Symbiotropin and within one week lost three pounds. Continued weight loss of three pounds per week throughout first cycle. Patient reported increased energy, increased sense of mental well-being, and deeper, more peaceful sleep. Skin appears softer and wrinkles are diminishing. Age spots diminishing.

L.C., Female, Age 48

History of severe cardiomyopathy and hypertension. Treatment with other therapies provided some improvement, however cardiovascular function continued to deteriorate. With Symbiotropin, her energy level immediately increased. Shortness of breath decreased dramatically. She reports increased energy and sense of well-being. Several of her medications have been eliminated, including an ACE inhibitor; she continues to improve rapidly.

B.N., Male, Age 63

Overweight, heavy smoker, with cardiovascular disease and pulmonary distress. Had been treated with chelation therapy with some improvement. Within four weeks of Symbiotropin therapy, breathing was greatly improved. Lessened shortness of breath allows him to exercise to a much greater extent. His blood pressure has been significantly reduced.

P.C., Female, Age 46

Heavy smoker with total hysterectomy performed in early 30's with subsequent hormone replacement therapy (HRT). HRT did not control her hot flashes, sleeplessness, and anxiety. With Symbiotropin therapy, she made dramatic improvement in these, and related menopausal symptoms to the extent that she was able to reduce her dose of estrogen and progestin while remaining symptom free. In addition, she reported improvement in other areas, including improved energy.

G.F., Female, Age 65

History of being depressed and overweight. No long-term success with previous treatments. After onset of Symbiotropin therapy, she experienced weight loss of 2 pounds per week. Reports more energy and tremendous improvement in mental outlook and anxiety.

L.J., Male, Age 55

Prior to Symbiotropin, this patient was overweight and experienced reduced energy and sexual potency. After onset of Symbiotropin, he has reported deeper and sounder sleep at night, which has eliminated his need for napping during the day. He has improved stamina and is able to exercise more vigorously. He reports significant improvement in sexual potency and has experienced continued weight loss.

"I weighed 300 lbs. and had been on insulin for almost five years... I was using a total of 175 units of 70/30 insulin everyday... my doctor added some glucophage... over the last two months I used Symbiotropin 5 nights a week, lost 50 lbs, and dropped insulin requirements to only 10 units a day!

I'm going to keep using [Symbiotropin]... I was on glucophage before & it didn't help. I know what is causing my improvement. Thank you!"

-D.J.

66————————————————————————

Now I have an overall healthy appearance and feeling of well-being.

– L.M. (Male, Age 75)

I have been on the Symbiotropin for the past four months... I have so much more energy now, I feel younger, I look younger, I have less pains... I appreciate the difference it has made in my life.

– R.B., Male

Thank you so much for suggesting the Symbiotropin. I have been on the product for three months, I have never felt better. My energy level is way up, my age spots are gone, I feel great...

– R.S., Male

————————————————————————99

*"Happiness is good health
and a bad memory."*
– Ingrid Bergman

CHAPTER FIVE

LOOKING YOUNGER
AND FEELING YOUNGER

By Dr. L.E. Dorman

As an osteopathic physician, I have been educated in techniques of treating a variety of influences on disease with a focus on structural manipulation. Examples of osteopathic procedures include the realignment of the cranium in a young child to assist in overcoming growth retardation and the effects of spinal manipulation on relieving knee pain. For me, understanding these and related concepts comes with the inherent acceptance that all areas of the body are interactive and while we may choose to isolate and treat diseases symptomatically, we will attain better results when we treat the body as a whole. As I continually strive to practice medicine with this as my guideline, I am assured that I am on the right path.

In the practice of nutrition and preventive medicine, I have observed unsurpassed improvements in a variety of disease states for which there otherwise seems to be no effective treatment.

I have seen the disparity in the response of patients who are treated similarly with nutrients and medication, but whose dietary and exercise habits differ. The results of long term exposure to a diet high in fat and refined carbohydrates are clear: insulin resistance, high blood pressure, increased body fat, fatigue, heart disease, high cholesterol, arthritis, and resistance to treatment. In researching growth hormone, I found these to be the precise areas that consistently improve with GH therapy.

I have long recognized the role of hormone replacement in deterring the aging process, and it has become clear to me that restoring growth hormone and IGF-1 ought to be a primary focus in HRT. In the replacement of any hormone, it is important for me to use a natural hormone rather than a synthetic one and to mimic the body's own production of that hormone in terms of quantity and frequency of release. Considering these parameters as part of a GH therapy that I would implement into my practice, I realized that it made a lot more sense to use a natural secretagogue rather than injections for the following reasons:

- *Natural:* Secretagogues stimulate the body's own growth hormone to be released, whereas injections utilize synthesized growth hormone.
- *Quantity & Frequency*: Symbiotropin enhances the existing pulsatile secretions of GH, while injections take the place of these secretions.
- *Conversion to IGF-1*: This process is affected by liver & pancreatic function, which are addressed by pharmaceutical sugars in Symbiotropin. Injections do not address this.
- *Side Effects:* Symbiotropin consists of all natural

ingredients, reducing the likelihood of side effects. Injections can cause many side effects, especially at higher doses.

- *Compliance:* Many patients find it difficult to inject themselves daily. Symbiotropin is delivered in a drinkable form. Injections must also be kept at low temperatures until use; this is not always practical.
- *Cost:* GH injections cost $800 - $1,200/month. Symbiotropin costs about $125.00 - $200.00/month.

The Insulin – Hormone Replacement Connection

While most physicians today are familiar with recognizing and treating hormone deficiency, there is generally a disregard for the complex interaction that all hormones have with one another. Insulin is a hormone that greatly affects the secretion and response to estrogen, growth hormone, progesterone, and thyroid hormone—and it is controlled largely by the diet, but not entirely. The aging process results in a declining ability to manage insulin and other hormones. Hence, the ideal anti-aging hormone therapy would include insulin management in a way that addresses insulin production and receptor sites. If insulin is not regulated, much higher dose of hormones—like estrogen—must be used to attain the desired response. This concept applies to the interaction of most replacement hormones that I am familiar with—the broader range of hormones that are being replaced, the lower the required dose for each of them.

For the most part, hormone replacement therapy (HRT) has proven to be quite effective in reversing symptoms associated with deficiency, but there are a significant number of patients who have a limited response. A good example of this is a female patient in her mid-forties who had a full hysterectomy in her early thirties and had been suffering from severe hot flashes, depression, and painful vaginal dryness. By the time she came to me, she had already been treated by many physicians with nearly every combination of hormones imaginable, but to no avail. By using natural hormones rather than the synthetic ones that she had been exposed to, we were able to improve her condition, but it seemed that we couldn't eliminate her symptoms entirely. Then we introduced Symbiotropin into her protocol. Within a few days she reported a complete disappearance of her depressive symptoms and a dramatic decrease in the intensity of her hot flashes. Within two weeks she had completely overcome all of her symptoms that she had suffered from for so many years, including the painful vaginal dryness. Did this seemingly miraculous recovery occur solely due to stimulation of growth hormone and IGF-1? Not exactly.

The methods by which Symbiotropin has its action include insulin regulation and control of blood glucose, which are both essential to GH release. Excess insulin and blood sugar inhibit the ability of hormones like estrogen to get into the cell and perform their function. This type of resistance to hormone therapy is often addressed by using superphysiologic doses—which go beyond replacement of a deficient hormone. From clinical experience, patients who do not fully respond to physiologic doses of HRT have outward symptoms of blood sugar imbalance, including the following:

- Difficulty getting from one meal to the next

- Fatigue, especially in the mid-afternoon

- Craving of sweets

- Excessive carbohydrate intake

- Dizziness and/or shakiness between meals

- Awakening to hunger in the middle of the night

- High or low blood glucose levels

- Diabetes

Patients with these symptoms are generally excellent candidates for Symbiotropin therapy.

Diabetic patients are easy to monitor for immediate response to Symbiotropin because glucose levels are monitored frequently. These patients have demonstrated remarkable glucose stability within the first few weeks of therapy. This is true even for those who are medicated, but who continue to have uncontrolled diabetes. I have observed patients who have ongoing problems with glucose levels that fluctuate daily, often reaching 250 – 350. One patient, a 64-year old male had worked with his endocrinologist for years, adjusting dosages and changing drugs, yet his blood sugar was consistently reaching 275 – 300. After 2 weeks of Symbiotropin, his blood sugar was peaking at 120; this response remained consistent to the extent that he is able to use lower doses of his medication while controlling his blood sugar in a way that previously seemed impossible.

The profound results that have been observed in controlling hyper and hypoglycemia are an interesting contrast to the known resistance to hGH injections that is normally experienced by these patients. As Jamieson has pointed out, healthy pancreatic function is necessary for the proper formation of IGF-1—in addition, glucose and insulin must be circulating at low levels in order for GH to be released. Addressing insulin resistance and insulin production seems to be not only a necessary component of GH stimulation, but a profound means of controlling blood sugar as well. With insulin playing a central role in the management of so many different hormones, it's no wonder that we are observing so many far reaching effects on menopausal symptoms, high blood pressure, heart disease, and other areas.

Before we go on to examine various areas of improvement that have been observed with Symbiotropin, it should be made clear that we set out to make these observations in the most objective manner possible. The patients were not instructed to monitor any symptoms that they had been experiencing at the onset of therapy. They were only told that their IGF-1 levels were found to be low, and that we would monitor changes in IGF-1 in response to Symbiotropin. I was amazed to find that patients were calling me within just a few days to report profound improvement in a variety of symptoms. They were reporting increased energy, flexibility, reduced pain from arthritis, and an overall improvement in the sense of well-being. The areas that I will focus on here are those in which I have observed consistent improvement. The following areas apply to diseases that afflict many people, and though I cannot suggest that Symbiotropin is a "cure" for these maladies—the results cannot be ignored.

Heart Disease & High Blood Pressure

My practice includes the use of EDTA chelation therapy with patients who have mild to advanced heart disease. Most of these patients are working closely with a cardiologist and many of them have severely impaired cardiovascular function to the extent that they have difficulty with simple exercises like walking. Reducing the plaque in the arteries is helpful, but with an unconditioned heart they often cannot perform simple tasks without shortness of breath. The results of Symbiotropin have been profound in this area. While a large number of patients have reported improved energy, perhaps the most profound stories are of those with heart disease who are suddenly able to not only walk across the room without running out of breath, but who are able to begin more intense heart strengthening exercises as well.

Studies that we have referred to previously suggest that hGH injections elicit a significant improvement in cardiac output. This may be due to the supportive role that IGF-1 plays in strengthening muscle tissue, but the effects of Symbiotropin seem to go beyond this effect in ways that are not fully understood. For instance, many patients with impaired pulmonary function and emphysema have reported rapid improvements in lung capacity and subsequent increase in stamina.

A 63-year old male who is overweight and a heavy smoker with heart disease had undergone chelation therapy and experienced some improvement, but when he was given Symbiotropin he had a marked increase in strength, endurance, and breathing capacity to the point that he can exercise daily. He has experienced increased muscle strength and reduced body fat as well.

Although emphysema is not typically associated with heart disease, the results in this area are significant in evaluating the total effect in improving cardiovascular function. A 67-year old male with chronic bronchitis and emphysema was non-responsive to other treatments, when he was given Symbiotropin he immediately experienced increased lung capacity, energy, and endurance. These results were not expected since I had not read any data indicating that other forms of growth hormone therapy had produced these results. Observations of increased lung capacity have been consistent despite the variety of influences on impaired pulmonary function, including smoking, allergies, emphysema, and bronchitis.

There are many influences on high blood pressure, including adrenaline, arterial plaque, and kidney function. Most patients are able to control the factors that affect their high blood pressure, while some have uncontrolled high blood pressure regardless of medication. It is in these cases of uncontrolled blood pressure that we have observed significant improvement. One such patient was using a combination of blood pressure medications, yet it was not uncommon for his blood pressure to reach 170/130 on a daily basis. After just a few weeks of Symbiotropin, he was able to maintain consistently controlled levels of 120/70 to 130/80.

Angina can be a frightening experience and a hindrance to heart-strengthening exercises. A 64-year old patient with advanced heart disease and daily chest pain onset with even mild exertion reported complete cessation of chest pain within 24 hours of the first dose of Symbiotropin. I choose this among other examples of improvement in angina because it suggests mechanisms of action that go beyond strengthening of the heart muscle, which would normally occur over a much longer period of time.

Arthritis & Musculoskelatal Improvement

This is another area that I had not anticipated to find the consistent improvement that we did. Nevertheless, the results couldn't be ignored. Patients have reported flexibility that they had not experienced in over 30 years, with several patients describing themselves to have an easier time getting out of bed in the morning. Those with arthritis reported significant reduction in pain. Many were able to recover from muscular injuries and pain from exercise much more efficiently. We observed increased range of motion in the joints and increased muscular strength. A few of my patients who had fibromyalgia, a condition that involves chronic muscular pain, had significantly reduced pain scores. The most fascinating and consistent reports were those of healing and reduced pain from old injuries. These include a patient who described pain in his shoulder that would wake him up at night and continue throughout the day—this 20-year old injury had caused constant pain that subsided after 8 weeks of Symbiotropin. An 83-year old man had a back injury that was more than 30-years old. He had such stiffness and pain that he could not bend over to tie his own shoes, but now he can touch his toes without bending his knees and without pain.

What are the common elements of these conditions and the changes that were observed? They all involve inflammation and degeneration, which both have many causative influences that may be affected by Symbiotropin. It is known that some forms of arthritis and fibromyalgia are directly affected by the integrity of the gastrointestinal lining. As we mentioned in the chapter, *The Facts*, studies indicate that growth hormone and the amino acid L-glutamine (an ingredient of Symbiotropin) are important factors in the growth and thickening of the digestive tract lining. This may be an important mechanism of action in pain reduction due to reduced leaking of inflammation-promoting substances from the digestive tract into the bloodstream. In addition, enhancing the digestive tract lining improves nutrient absorption, which may assist in healing of damaged tissues.

Nutrient absorption is not the end of the story. Once nutrients are absorbed they must be utilized in a way that will help to repair cells and the tissues that they support. Growth hormone is unique among hormones in that it stimulates growth by directly targeting tissues, rather than endocrine organs. The insulin-like effects of IGF-1 as well as the insulin regulating effects of GH therapy play an integral role in the growth and reparation of tissues. Insulin transports glucose, proteins, and fats into the cell where they are used for energy and cell replication. By improving insulin utilization, we inherently promote healing. When we add the complimentary effects of growth hormone and IGF-1, the results are truly amazing.

It should be noted that the mechanisms that are described here are a sharp contrast to the action of anti-inflammatory drugs (steroids and NSAIDS). These medications reduce inflammation, but at the expense of wearing away the digestive tract lining and breaking down collagen in the joints. They offer an effective and immediate reduction in pain, but they do not repair tissues. In fact, they work to accelerate damage to tissues that are causing inflammation— creating a long-term dependence and worsening of the condition. There are supportive nutrients that can supply the raw materials for rebuilding this damaged tissue, but without the proper hormonal stimulation results may be limited.

Insomnia

Best-selling books on melatonin have shed light on the importance of sleep in controlling the aging process. Melatonin, referred to as the sleep hormone, is produced according to a similar circadian rhythm as growth hormone, where they are both released primarily at night. Some melatonin researchers are now suggesting that some of the anti-aging benefits of melatonin may come from its growth hormone enhancing properties. Both hormones are produced in declining amounts as we age—to the extent that many elderly people have difficulty sleeping and do not have efficient rest.

Most patients, including those who didn't previously describe difficulty in sleeping, have reported improvements in their ability to fall asleep, stay asleep, attain deeper and more efficient sleep, and experience more vivid dreams. They have reported feeling more refreshed upon awaking and having more energy during the morning hours. We have not measured melatonin levels in these patients to determine a change, but there is clearly an improvement in sleep. From experience, melatonin supplementation produces mixed results—this does not seem to be the case with Symbiotropin, which seems to work consistently in this area.

Insulin regulation plays a role in sleep patterns as well. Hypoglycemia, or low blood sugar, tends to occur at night simply because we don't eat while we are sleeping. When blood glucose levels drop, adrenaline is released as a secondary energy source. As a stimulatory hormone, a release of adrenaline at night can result in a variety of outcomes, from initiating lighter and less efficient sleep, to causing night sweats and sleeplessness. The management of insulin that occurs with Symbiotropin may be a significant mechanism of action that helps to improve sleep by reducing the incidence of nocturnal hypoglycemia.

Weight Control

I refer to control rather that loss because we have observed consistent increase in muscle mass and significant decrease in body fat, which, together, do not always produce weight loss. This process often begins within the first week of Symbiotropin therapy where patients have experienced weight loss of up to 7 pounds. The majority of overweight patients maintain a loss of 2-3 pounds per week. At the same time, the increased strength, energy, and endurance allow them to perform higher intensity workouts—thereby increasing muscle mass and raising the base metabolism.

As is the case with so many other areas of improvement with Symbiotropin, insulin regulation plays a central role. In our chapter on Diet & Exercise we will go into greater detail on things that you can do to enhance this process. IGF-1 and growth hormone are both known to elicit lypolisis (fat burning) and building of muscle tissue. Some nutritionists and doctors still subscribe to the philosophy that fat storage is based purely upon the difference between calories going in (diet) and calories going out (exercise). Although this is an important principal, many people find it to be frustrating and insulting. You don't have to look far (perhaps as far as the nearest mirror) to find a person who cannot maintain the body composition that they could previously, despite the fact that they have not changed their diet or exercise habits. Even worse, many people continue to store more fat even while consuming fewer calories and doing more exercise. This unfortunate process takes place largely due to the hormonal changes that occur with age. The endocrine system is no longer maintaining the same metabolic rate. This can often be observed by a decline in body temperature and/or reduced energy and endurance. By restoring growth hormone and IGF-1, we are not only directly restoring our ability to burn fat, but we are also helping to restore proper function of endocrine organs, like the thyroid, that maintain our metabolism.

Hair, Skin, and Nails

Growth hormone and IGF-1 stimulate the growth of hair, nails, and skin. Several patients have reported rapid growth of nails and hair, to the point that the have to visit the barber shop more frequently. Many have reported thicker and healthier hair and nails as well. But let's get right to the point—most of us want to know how to get rid of those wrinkles. This is a process that is more likely to occur with long term use and with the other supportive nutrients. However, we have observed significant reduction in wrinkles in men and women within as little as 4 weeks. I have seen patients in their 70's and 80's transform their complexion from gaunt, colorless, and wrinkled to plump, healthy, and smoother in a very short period of time. Yet, I have seen others who don't seem to show such dramatic signs of improvement. What's the difference?

Many of my patients are using nutritional protocols that include large doses of vitamin C, bioflavanoids, and amino acids like proline and lysine, which are components of collagen—the "glue" for skin cells that help to maintain firmness and strength. Other patients are not supplementing with these important raw materials for collagen synthesis and have had a history of smoking and excess sun exposure, which breaks down collagen. There appears to be a difference in the way that these two groups of people respond to Symbiotropin in terms of wrinkle reduction, but there may be other influences that are not fully understood. It will be interesting to see if, over a longer period of time, we will see more consistent smoothing of skin.

Sex Drive

Both male and female patients have reported improvement in libido and duration of intercourse. The response to sex hormones—like testosterone—are enhanced with GH therapy, which would explain the increase in sex drive for both sexes. In addition, men will benefit from increased circulation and the effect that this has on maintaining erection.

Testing and Monitoring

At this point, Symbiotropin has only been used under the advice and supervision of a physician. It has been used only in patients who demonstrate IGF-1 levels below 350 with monitoring every 4 - 8 weeks. Our results have shown flucuating IGF-1 levels in the first four weeks of use with increases of IGF-1 reaching over 200% and averaging over 18%. In the next four weeks of use, changes in IGF-1 tend to be more stable—peaking just over 100% and averaging 24%. By the twelfth week of use (the end of the first cycle) we have observed the most consistent symptomatic improvements and increases in IGF-1, with an average increase of over 30%, to date. Interestingly, we had a few patients that had temporarily reduced IGF-1 levels, but for the most part these patients still exhibited symptomatic improvement. In a clinical enviroment it is probably not necessary to test IGF-1 more frequently than before and after each 12-week cycle of Symbiotropin.

Average increase in IGF-1 throughout first 12-week cycle of Symbiotropin.

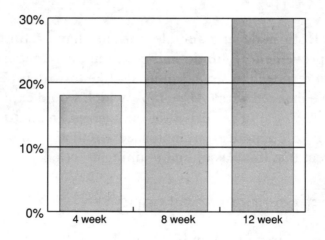

All patients included in this study had initial IGF-1 levels below 350. Several patients with higher IGF-1 levels, including athletes, were given Symbiotropin and reported marked improvements in strength, stamina, and body composition. The changes observed in many of these patients indicates that Symbiotropin may work by sensitizing IGF-1 and insulin receptors. For example, an avid runner in her mid-forties was maintaining IGF-1 levels of 403, but she exhibited signs of low growth hormone such as unexplained weight gain and fatigue. Within weeks of beginning Symbiotropin therapy, she began to lose significant amounts of body fat while improving her energy and stamina without a significant increase in IGF-1. Body builders who have previously used GH injections have reported more rapid increase in muscle mass and definition with Symbiotropin.

The results of patient self-assessments indicate symptomatic response to Symbiotropin within the first four weeks in all patients, with continued improvement between the fourth and twelfth week. Improved energy, endurance, and body composition were among the most frequently reported improvements within the first four weeks. New hair growth, restoration of hair color, thickening of skin, and disappearance of skin discoloration generally occurred between the eighth and twelfth weeks, with continued improvement beyond the twelve week term. It should be noted that the results of this patient self-assessment are not adjusted for areas that did not apply to each individual.

Patients % Reported Improvement with Symbiotropin

Area of Assessment	Month Three
Endurance & Body Composition	
Muscle Strength	58%
Muscle Size	42%
Fat Reduction	68%
Overall Energy	74%
Exercise Tolerance	58%
Exercise Endurance	68%
Hair & Skin	
Skin Texture	47%
Skin Thickness	32%
Skin Elasticity	26%
Wrinkle Disappearance	37%
New Hair Growth	47%
Healing & Immunity	
Healing of old injuries	26%
Healing of other injuries	21%
Healing Capacity	21%
Back & Joint Flexibility	37%
Resistance to Common Illness	47%
Sexual Function	
Sexual Potency/Frequency	32%
Duration of Penile Erection	44%
Frequency of Nighttime Urination	66%
Mental Function	
Mental Energy & Clarity	53%
Emotional Stability	42%
Attitude Toward Life	37%
Memory	47%

Our experience with testing laboratories warrants the suggestion of using a laboratory that is experienced in the testing of IGF-1. This is a highly sensitive test in which blood samples must be kept frozen and handled properly. Allan Broughton, M.D., Director Antibody Assay Laboratories in Santa Ana, California (800-522-2611), established the first commercially available test for IGF-1 in 1979. My personal contact with him in the process of monitoring patients has been tremendously insightful as to the variability of IGF-1 assays when they are not performed in the proper environment.

We are publishing a continually updated guide for physicians who are using Symbiotropin. If your physician is not already familiar with this type of therapy, he/she may contact the publisher of this book for more information.

66

My fingernails have greatly improved. I have a healthier overall appearance, and my energy is greatly improved.

– M.M. (Female, Age 74)

99

"Never mistake motion for action."

– Ernest Hemmingway

CHAPTER SIX

OPTIMIZING hGH THERAPY WITH DIET AND EXERCISE

The importance of diet and exercise in optimizing growth hormone levels applies to those who elect growth hormone therapies as well as those who don't. Irregular insulin levels and lack of exercise are known to contribute to accelerated symptoms of aging like heart disease, obesity, and diabetes. The diet and exercise recommendations for boosting hGH help to control the endogenous factors of disease and aging as well as enhancing the effectiveness of hGH therapies. It is no coincidence that studies on the effects of exercise produce many of the same results as studies on growth hormone therapy, including increased bone density and muscle mass, reduction of cholesterol, blood pressure, and triglycerides, decreased body fat, and increased life expectancy. Exercise and dietary control of insulin both work to increase growth hormone secretion. Imagine the accelerated influence of combining proper diet, exercise and GH therapy. Many elderly people have limited strength and stamina that affects their ability to exert themselves to the point of making significant gains against heart disease and osteoporosis. Restoring growth hormone levels often increases their energy, strength and stamina so they are able to do exercises that previously seemed impossible. The proper dietary measures can help to enhance growth hormone release and the effects of IGF-1 so that better results are obtained more quickly.

We have repeatedly observed the remarkable influence that GH therapy has on increasing exercise potential. An 83-year-old patient with extremely limited mobility, arthritis, and stiffness had not been able to exercise, after one week on Symbiotropin he had the flexibility and reduced pain that allowed him to walk everyday and increase his tolerance for weight bearing exercise. The profound improvements in cardiovascular health described in the previous chapter are the most consistent contributors to improved exercise tolerance.

Many athletes who train heavily are known to maintain youthful levels of growth hormone right into their 50's, 60's, and 70's. We have had several reports of increased strength, stamina, and muscle mass with young athletes, but there is not enough data to draw any definitive conclusions or make recommendations for this application. However, test results with athletes whose initial IGF-1 were near optimal contributed to our conclusions that GH will not become over-stimulated in people who have close to optimal GH levels. Even the 8% increases in IGF-1 that have been observed with athletes on Symbiotropin can make a tremendous difference in the competitive edge of a body builder or athlete.

Growth hormone levels increase significantly when insulin levels are low, about four hours after a meal. It is at this point that the fat burning potential of GH tends to be at its daytime peak. But remember, the largest burst of GH is released during the early hours of sleep—hence, our evening eating habits are crucial to maximizing this nighttime secretion. By avoiding food during the last four hours before bedtime we may enhance circadian growth hormone release, and fat burning potential.

Symbiotropin and GH injections are often taken just before bedtime to enhance or mimic the circadian pulse of GH. In the case of secretagogues, the avoidance of food is important not only in suppressing insulin, but also in eliminating the competition of dietary proteins with amino acid peptides. The amino acid sequences in Symbiotropin are very targeted and delicate in their design—the introduction of other proteins and amino acids can interfere with receptors for these therapeutic peptides.

Clinically, we have found that most patients have difficulty in avoiding food four hours before bedtime. Many of us are so busy that we just don't get home in time to eat dinner before six, and other people are accustom to munching or drinking carbohydrates right up until bedtime. If snacking before bedtime is unavoidable, the morning is the next best time to use Symbiotropin therapy. Sleeping all night results in desirably low insulin levels because of the inherent fasting that takes place. In theory, using GH therapy at night after four hours of fasting is great, but as a matter of practicality we have found that morning doses of Symbiotropin are potentiated by nighttime fasting and produce excellent results. To maximize the morning dose, food and dietary supplements should be avoided for at least 1 – 2 hours after using Symbiotropin, and if possible, cardiovascular or weight resistance exercise should take place during this period of food avoidance. Many patients have reported such a profound increase in energy and endurance with Symbiotropin that they are able to do strenuous exercise without carbohydrate loading ahead of time, thus accelerating the fat burning process.

There have been several reports of carbohydrate cravings an hour or more after the ingestion of Symbiotropin—this is an exciting indicator that the product is working. The effect of raising growth hormone can be likened to the effects of exercise in several ways. As GH levels rise, insulin responds by mobilizing glucose and bringing it to cells, including muscle, as an energy source. Glucose demand from the cells stimulates the breakdown of glycogen and triglycerides (body fat) as secondary and tertiary sources of energy. This is the process that results in fat burning and muscle building during exercise. As every athlete knows, the body craves carbohydrates after a work out and replacing those exhausted carbohydrates and protein is essential to rebuilding muscle tissue that has been damaged by exertion. Just as it is in the case of exercise, it is important to coordinate carbohydrate and protein restoration with growth hormone therapy.

When we say that GH therapy mimics the effects of exercise, we are not suggesting that it negates the necessity of exercise. In fact, exercise is a potent growth hormone stimulator. Many athletes choose to use natural secretagogues before a work out, no matter what time of day, in order to enhance the bump in GH that comes from exercises like high-intensity running and weight lifting. For those of us who are not athletic, increasing growth hormone levels with injections or secretagogues often leads to the improved strength and energy that it takes to increase the intensity, and subsequent GH release, of the exercises that we're already doing. It's a two way street, growth hormone enhances exercise and exercise enhances growth hormone.

Growth Hormone Significantly Improves Body Composition:

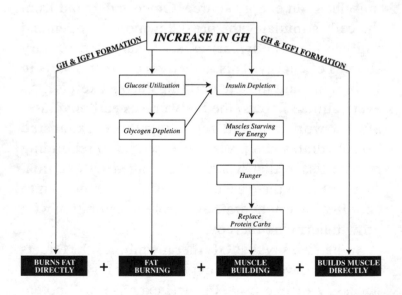

Remember, depending on a person's initial body composition and exercise habits, losing fat and gaining muscle with GH therapy may not result in weight loss, but it will result in better measurements. When we increase muscle mass, we increase our overall metabolism thereby contributing to our ability to burn more body fat and calories. Supporting the growth of muscle tissue with diet and exercise is an integral part of optimizing GH therapy. We have found the best results clinically when patients eat fruit or other healthy carbohydrates about an hour after taking Symbiotropin. In this way we are optimizing the interaction of growth hormone and insulin in order to maximize the increase in muscle mass. Insulin escorts carbohydrates (as glucose) and proteins into the cell to be used in fueling muscle and other tissues. The dietary guidelines of GH therapy are appropriate for all patients on GH therapy, even in the unavoidable absence of exercise.

The best carbohydrates to use as a replacement are those that will break down to glucose more slowly. You may refer to a glycemic index for specific values of certain foods, but as a rule consume complex carbohydrates combined with fiber and good fats. For instance, a breakfast that includes steel cut oats will offer more a more sustained glucose supply because they are higher in fiber than rolled oats. Adding raw ground flaxseeds supplies even more fiber along with beneficial omega-3 fatty acids which work to slow down the uptake of glucose into the bloodstream. Whole grains contain more fiber and are always a better choice than refined grains. These guidelines apply to snacks and meals throughout the day. Avoiding refined flours and simple carbohydrates helps to control insulin thereby optimizing GH secretion as well as response to many other hormones. In fact, studies of insulin controlling substances and calorie restrictive diets indicate that employing these guidelines will contribute to longevity.

Optimum GH Enhancing Routine

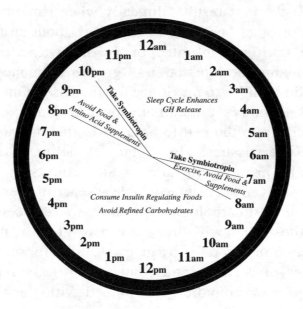

Certain supplements, like chromium picolinate, have been shown to have a regulatory effect on insulin thereby enhancing GH release. The following products may be used to enhance any GH protocol, but they may be especially important for diabetics or hypoglycemics, who may have a resistance to GH therapy.

Chromium Picolinate: A trace mineral that, according to researcher Dr. Gary Evans, helps insulin to fit into the cell better thereby overcoming insulin resistance and lowering circulating insulin and blood sugar. These processes are important in reducing fat storage, burning existing fat and promoting muscle growth. Research on chromium picolinate shows that it is consistently effective at doing all of the above, even in sedentary individuals. Suggested dose: 200 – 600 mcg/day.

Vanadium: A trace mineral that has an insulin-mimicking effect. Assists in utilization of blood glucose and subsequent management of insulin. Clinical experience shows that the a vanadyl complex is better absorbed and can be used in lower doses than other, more poorly absorbed forms like vanadyl sulfate. Recommended dose: 200 – 500 mcg/day.

Gymnema Sylvestre: This herb is used widely in India to treat blood sugar abnormalities. It contains a molecule that is so similar to glucose that it sits on sugar receptors, which helps to inhibit the release of glucose into the bloodstream and control insulin response. It is used as an aid in weight control and an inhibitor of sugar cravings, when applied directly to the tongue it will block the ability to taste anything sweet. Suggested use: standardized extract, 500 – 1000 mg. before meals.

Proteusterone: This herbal complex has a large part of its action in the support of liver, pancreatic, and adrenal function in ways that help to manage insulin and blood sugar. Clinical experience has shown an improved response in Symbiotropin therapy for diabetics who use Proteusterone at night. As an endocrine supplement, this product is designed to enhance any individual hormone therapy, and is used by many athletes to improve muscle growth and stamina. Suggested use: 1 – 3 tablets/day.

Studies show that there are specific exercises that are particularly effective at stimulating GH release. As we share them with you, it is important to point out that any exercise will help to enhance the effects of growth hormone. The following exercises are used specifically help to increase GH release and have a rate of effectiveness that, for the most part, is proportionate to the intensity of the exercise.

EXERCISE	INTENSITY	HGH SECRETION
Running (Women)	High	266% increase in trough levels 75% increase in daily secretion
Running (Men)	Moderate	0% – Moderate
Stationary Bike (both sexes)	High	166% increase
Stationary Bike (both sexes)	Moderate	166% increase
Weight Training (both sexes)	85% MLC*	400% increase
Weight Training (both sexes)	70% MLC*	300% increase
Weight Training (both sexes)	Moderate – High	Immediate & Sustained increase
Treadmill (both sexes)	High	Increased GH Pulse

* MLC = Maximal Lift Capacity, the maximum amount of weight able to be lifted once.

All weight-training exercises are effective promoters of GH release, but those that involve the use of high-resistance and major muscle groups tend to be the most effective. Applying maximum effort to fewer repetitions of squats, leg presses, deadlifts, overhead presses, bench presses, standing curls, and leg curls will optimize your results. In addition, go to MLC for one rep of each of these exercises no more than once a week to create an additional boost of GH. If you are not experienced with weight training, please work with your physician to determine your physical condition and work with a qualified personal trainer who can teach you proper technique.

66————————————————————

Defects in my skin are disappearing and my skin is much smoother. I am much happier, more alert, and thinking more calmly. I am sleeping much longer (more restful). My blood pressure has come way down; I am taking 1/4 of my medication now. My insulin units have been reduced from 65 units to 10–15 units per day. I have more stamina and my legs no longer hurt when I walk.

– D.B. (Female, Age 75)

————————————————————99

"Aging isn't for sissies."

– Katherine Hepburn

CHAPTER SEVEN

INTERACTION OF GROWTH HORMONE WITH OTHER HORMONES

As our knowledge of various anti-aging hormones has expanded, we have continued to gain an understanding of the variety of ways that these substances work. The clinical experience of experts in the field of hormone replacement therapy (HRT) concur with our own data that when a wider array of hormones is administered, lower doses of each individual hormone can be used. This is particularly desirable in the case of high activity estrogens and testosterone, which carry risks along with their benefits when used at super-physiologic doses. The goal in the replacement of *any* hormone is to approach and maintain physiologic levels— otherwise we are second-guessing nature. As we have learned more about the GH stimulating effects of DHEA, testosterone, and estrogen – the pressing question on the minds of many researchers is, "Are some of the observable anti-aging effects of these hormones occurring as a result of secondary GH stimulation?"

It is important here to distinguish between the use of natural and synthetic hormones. Most physicians in the U.S. are familiar with the use of synthetic patented drugs like Premarin as an estrogen replacement, Provera as a "progesterone" replacement, and methyl-testosterone as a testosterone replacement. These synthetic drugs are not the same as their counterparts that are manufactured by the body, hence they are not recognized or metabolized as such. Non-patented (therefore less profitable and less promoted) versions of these natural hormones are readily available and generally less expensive. Some clinicians argue against using natural hormones because of absorption problems, but this is a disputable point since all of these hormones are available in pharmaceutical delivery systems, which transcend the limiting use of capsules. In addition, there are a variety of botanical substances that support and the action of a variety of hormones. Let's look at the effects of some of the hormones that diminish with age, and the options that are available in replacing them.

Estrogen

The term "estrogen" represents an entire family of substances with similar chemical structures that bind to estrogen receptors in the body. There are three types of estrogen produced by the body, estrone, estradiol, and estriol. Although men produce estrogen in limited amounts, it is associated with the development of secondary sexual characteristics in women and is used primarily as a hormone replacement in females. Estrogen is necessary for the proper maintenance of bone tissue through inhibition of osteoclasts. It has been shown to reduce the risk of heart disease and control LDL cholesterol. Maintaining stable estrogen levels is important in controlling hot flashes, mood swings, and other symptoms associated with menopause. Estrogen has a stimulatory effect on GH and vise versa. Estrogen is available in synthetic form and is commonly prescribed as Premarin or Estrace, which contain high-activity estradiol and estrone. These products are contraindicated in women with a history of sex cell related cancers. Their side effects include weight gain, possible increased risk of breast cancer, mood swings, depression, headaches, lowered thyroid function, and increased risk of stroke. In Europe, the most widely prescribed form of estrogen is estriol. It does not have the contraindications and side effects that the other forms of estrogen have. It is even used in women who have breast cancer because it is thought to have a protective effect against this devastating disease. Physiologically, the presence of estriol has a rate limiting effect on the production of the high activity estrogens that may otherwise cause symptoms of PMS and other signs of estrogen dominance. Many herbalists and naturally oriented physicians recommend phyto-estrogens from plant sources like dong quai, licorice, and soy. Concentrated forms of these plant estrogens appear to be effective in the treatment and prevention of sex cell cancers—the NIH continues to conduct research in this area.

Estrasterone is a natural estrogen supplement. By combining the only known plant source of estriol with other phyto-estrogens and herbal progesterone support, the product offers the same estrogen activity of .625 mg. (the most commonly prescribed dose) of Premarin without the long list of side effects. Studies on the effects of one tablet per day of Estrasterone indicate a 92% reduction in hot flashes as well 88% - 90% improvement in other symptoms of menopause, such as headaches, depressive moods, and sleep disturbances—all within three weeks.

Progesterone

Progesterone refers to one specific molecule as it is produced by the body, however the term is often misused to describe compounds that are actually progestins, like the prescription drug Provera. Progesterone, used primarily in women, promotes the growth of bone tissue, and in many ways counterbalances the unwanted effects of estrogen dominance like bloating, cramping, mood swings, depression, and headaches. Progesterone also facilitates thyroid function and has a protective effect against many sex cell cancers. While natural progesterone is known to be virtually free of side effects (it is produced in very large amounts by the placenta during pregnancy) and not directly related to the development of secondary sexual characteristics, this is not the case with synthetic progestins. Progestins do not stimulate bone tissue growth, nor do they, with the exception of endometrial cancer protection, provide the many benefits of natural progesterone. In addition, progestins have many side effects including compounding the increased risk of breast cancer associated with synthetic estrogens, inhibiting thyroid function, causing weight gain, depression, and headaches. Why do most doctors continue to prescribe synthetic progestins? Because natural progesterone is not patented, and it is not well-promoted. Progesterone is a precursor for most other adrenal hormones as well as a growth hormone stimulant. Clinical experience shows that lower amounts of progesterone are required with the use of GH therapy. As both GH and progesterone are effective stimulators of bone growth, it makes sense to use them in concert with natural estrogen in the treatment of osteoporosis.

Natural progesterone has absorption problems when taken orally that are overcome with the use of topical delivery. Dermasterone is used in several natural progesterone products that employ transdermal (across the skin) sustained release delivery systems to more closely mimic the manner in which progesterone is released throughout the day.

Testosterone

Testosterone has been traditionally recognized as a male sex hormone, as it is involved in male secondary sexual characteristics. It is important for both men and women in stabilizing mood, promoting sex drive, maintaining bone density, burning fat, and building muscle. The effects of lowered levels of testosterone, which occur in aging men, are collectively referred to as andropause. Symptoms of andropause include weight gain, reduced sex drive, difficulty in maintaining erection, osteoporosis (uncommon), and depression. In women, low testosterone levels may cause vaginal dryness, depression, and lack of sex drive. Testosterone is thought to be the most potent GH stimulant of all sex hormones.

Testosterone is commonly prescribed as a patch or gel and is known to have absorption problems when administered orally, but with the proper delivery, these problems may be overcome. There are botanical products that contain testosterone support as well as plant steroids that mimic its effects. Testrasterone incorporates a proprietary delivery system with active glandulars, and botanical testosterone support.

DHEA

This mildly androgenic hormone is produced by the adrenal glands of men and women. DHEA is a precursor to other adrenal hormones and diminishes with age in both sexes. Animal studies conducted with DHEA indicate that it is a promoter of longevity. Not only is DHEA a growth hormone stimulant— but the mechanisms that control its production, particularly insulin regulation, are related to those that control the secretion of GH. DHEA is available in two molecular forms, free DHEA and DHEA sulfate. Oral absorption of free DHEA is superior to the sulfate form, but can vary depending on particle size. The use of micronized DHEA insures optimal absorption and produces a predictable outcome in terms of blood levels.

As is the case with other hormones, more DHEA is not better. Super-physiologic levels of DHEA can overwhelm the adrenal glands and cause excess production of estrogen, testosterone, and other hormones while creating down-regulation and a dependence on DHEA. Clinically, we have found that the use of a uniformly released DHEA that is dispersed in microgram amounts over a twelve-hour period (zero-order release) prevents the excess production of secondary hormones. Additionally, the use of supportive botanicals and adrenal glandulars often allows the required dose of DHEA to become diminished over time.

Thyroid Hormone

Thyroid function diminishes with age not only because of declining thyroid hormone production, but because of the inhibited response of cells to thyroid hormone. Hence, many people who have thyroid deficiencies are not able to detect them strictly with the use of a blood test. The thyroid regulates metabolism and body temperature and affects every cell in the body. Symptoms of thyroid deficiency include low body temperature, fatigue, mood swings, depression, unexplained weight gain, irregular menstrual cycles, dry skin and hair, and brittle nails. Raising GH has a profound effect on normalizing thyroid function, as does the use of progesterone and natural estriol. Many patients require lower doses of thyroid medication, or eventually none at all, when a variety of natural hormone therapies is introduced. T4 (Synthroid) is the most commonly prescribed form of thyroid medication, but many people are not able to respond symptomatically due to other hormone imbalances, nutritional deficiencies, or autoimmune influences. As these influences are difficult to fully evaluate, Armour's glandular-based thyroid is often a better choice.

Melatonin

All the rage of best-selling books and media talk show hosts, melatonin has maintained its status as one of the hottest anti-aging hormones on the market. Researchers have indicated that some benefits of melatonin may be due to its stimulatory effect on GH release. And some caution against using it on a daily basis, especially for those who may not be deficient. It has become abundantly clear that growth hormone therapy induces deeper and more efficient sleep. Patients consistently experience more vivid dreams with the use of Symbiotropin, and others who have had chronic sleep disorders have reported overcoming them shortly after the onset of Symbiotropin therapy. Melatonin probably has its role as a replacement hormone when used intermittently. Further testing would help us to understand if Symbiotropin has a measurable effect on melatonin that is correlative to symptomatic improvement.

66—————————————————————

My blood pressure has gone down and stayed down since being on Symbiotropin.

— S.B. (Female, Age 45)

—————————————————————**99**

*"I don't want to achieve immortality
through my work; I want to achieve
immortality through not dying."*

– Woody Allen

CHAPTER EIGHT

HOW DO hGH THERAPIES

MEASURE UP?

We have reviewed the studies on hGH injections and provided the details of a variety of ways to increase your own GH secretion through diet, exercise, and the proper natural secretagogues. Now, the ultimate question in evaluating the differences among these various modes of GH therapy becomes, "Which GH therapy is right for me?"

Here are some areas of comparison to consider in answering this question:

	SYMBIOTROPIN	GH INJECTIONS
Dosage Form	Drink	Injection
Side Effects	Rare*	Several*
Cost per month	$120 – $200	$800 – $2,000
Effectiveness	Within 30 days	60 days +
Availability	Readily	Restricted
Convenience	Easy to travel with	Must be refridgerated
Allergies	Rare	Somewhat Common
Biocompatability	Natural	Synthetic
Support of IGF1 formation	Yes	No
Contraindications	Rare	A few***

* The only side effect observed with Symbiotropin was a mild allergic reaction (skin rash) to citric acid.
** Side effects of GH injections include musculoskelatal pain and edema.
*** Contraindicated in cancer patients and those with existing edema (swelling) of unknown case.

The top priority in replacing hormones should be to do it as naturally as possible. With this as a primary objective, growth hormone replacement is ideal because, unlike other hormones, it continues to be produced in significant amounts right into old age. So rather than replacing GH, our primary focus is on stimulating its release. The diet and exercise recommendations that we have outlined for promoting GH release are just as important in preventing symptoms of aging as they are in treating them. We have repeatedly observed patients who are able to maintain youthful IGF-1 levels well into their 70's just by maintaining a consistent adherence to a GH promoting lifestyle. But this is not the case for everyone.

> ## *Many factors affect the ability of the body to release growth hormone and form IGF-1, including:*
>
> ## Physical and Emotional stress
> ## Chronic disease Liver dysfunction
> ## Pancreatic dysfunction
> ## Poor diet
> ## Genetic predispostion

In addition, by the time many people consider themselves to be candidates for growth hormone therapy, they have reached a point of depletion that they are not able to tolerate the intensity of a GH promoting exercise program. This can often be overcome by kick-starting the body with Symbiotropin or injections.

Step 1: Measure your IGF-1 levels.

IGF-1 levels are relatively stable, so you do not need to be concerned about what time of day or month to measure them. Remember, when we talk about the importance of growth hormone therapy, we are referring to restoring IGF-1 to youthful levels. Before using any GH therapy, aside from diet and exercise, a deficiency must be established. A general consensus exists among scientists and physicians that any person regardless of age, whose IGF-1 levels are found to be below 100ng/ml, is considered to be GH deficient. However, the caveat is that the normal IGF-1 level does not exclude the diagnosis of growth hormone deficiency. This is the case for approximately 80% of the population over the age of 40 years old. From clinical experience, deficiency is often found in younger patients with hysterectomy, chronic fatigue syndrome, difficulty in weight control, chronic diseases, and HIV. The existence of any of these conditions warrants the measurement of IGF-1 levels.

In establishing an IGF-1 deficiency, a first course of action may include Symbiotropin in combination with diet and exercise therapy. The standard recommendation is two tablets/ day for five days on and two days off intervals for three months, then repeat the cycle if necessary. This protocol may be varied according to test results and symptomatic changes, as follows:

IF IGF-1 LEVELS ARE (IN NG/DL):

Below 100: Use double dose of Symbiotropin (morning and night) until levels reach 200, or until symptoms stabilize. Then continue with single dose (2 tablets/day) as maintenance.

100-200: Follow standard dosing. If symptomatic improvement is not progressing as expected, double dose for 1-2 weeks, then maintain at single dose (2 tablets/day).

200-350: Follow standard dosing, be sure to re-check levels after each 3-month cycle to evaluate the next stage of your protocol.

350+: Generally, this does not represent a deficiency. It is recommended to follow dietary and exercise recommendations to maintain these levels. The exceptions are:

- If you have reached these levels with the use of Symbiotropin, you will probably need to maintain this ideal level with continued single dosing at three month on and one month off intervals. Keep re-testing every 3-4 months.

- If your initial IGF-1 levels appear normal, but you are exhibiting other symptoms of GH deficiency—you may not be responding adequately to your circulating IGF-1. Follow one half or single dosing of Symbiotropin for a three-month cycle. then evaluate symptomatic improvement in order to determine continuing use.

Baseline clinical testing of IGF-1 levels are not necessary. Because of the proven safety and effectiveness of Symbiotropin, it is not necessary to do rigorous blood work or other lab tests as they are costly and an unecessary expense.Symbiotropin is not a hormone or drug but truly a revolutionary nutraceutical

Step 2: Evaluate your lifestyle.

No matter what your IGF-1 levels are, the lifestyle that you choose will make all the difference in maintaining and increasing your IGF-1. Whether you are using injections or Symbiotropin, your diet and exercise habits will potentiate your response.

- Are you currently exercising 4 days/week or more?
- In your current state of health, are you able to begin a GH promoting exercise program?
- Does your diet/supplement program resemble the one that is suggested for promotion of GH?
- Are you willing to make changes in your diet in order to more effectively promote GH secretion?

If your answer to the second question is no, keep asking yourself this key question throughout the term of your growth hormone therapy - you may be surprised at how quickly the answer will become, "Yes!"

Step 3: Evaluate your symptoms.

As scientists, we are familiar with the importance of blood tests in measuring response, but the most important thing to monitor is symptomatic improvement. After all, what difference does any therapy make if the patient doesn't feel better? The patient self-assessment that is provided in the following chapter is an essential part of growth hormone therapy. It is important for you and your physician to monitor the rate of change in various areas in order to determine an ongoing treatment protocol.

❝

I am sleeping much better at night. Blood pressure is normal after being borderline high for several years.

– JH. (Male, Age 65)

❞

> *"Being on the tightrope is living;*
> *everything else is waiting."*
>
> – Karl Wallenda

CHAPTER NINE

YOUR MONTHLY JOURNAL

The following Patient Self-Assessment is used by physicians to help them monitor patients' response to Symbiotropin. Many symptomatic changes that occur with growth hormone therapy take place over weeks for one patient and months for another. By keeping track of each three-month cycle of Symbiotropin, you and your physician will have an easier time to track changes that are occurring over longer periods of time. Please feel free to talk with your physician about adding other areas of assessment to this list that may suit your particular concerns. Remember that this list is a guideline composed of the most commonly reported areas of improvement; it is not a list of expectations.

Patient Self-Assessment: Effects of Symbiotropin at One Month Intervals

Name_____ Age_____

Doctor's Name _____

Cycle #_____ Dates of Previous 3 Month Cycles_____

Initial IGF1 before current cycle (please include units) _____

Initial IGF1 before all cycles (please include units) _____

IGF1 level after current cycle (please include units) _____

Comments_____

_____

_____

Please complete the following assessment at one month intervals throughout this three month cycle of Symbiotropin™ in order to assist you and your physician in monitoring response. Please rate your level of improvement in the following areas on a scale of 1 – 3.

1 = No Change   2 = Somewhat Improved
3 = Greatly Improved   N/A = Not Applicable

Please comment on these or any other areas where you have noticed symptomatic changes.

Area of Assessment	Month One	Month Two	Month Three
Endurance & Body Composition			
Muscle Strength			
Muscle Size			
Fat Reduction			
Overall Energy			
Exercise Tolerance			
Exercise Endurance			
Hair & Skin			
Skin Texture			
Skin Thickness			
Skin Elasticity			
Wrinkle Disappearance			
New Hair Growth			
Healing & Immunity			
Healing of old injuries			
Healing of other injuries			
Healing Capacity			
Back & Joint Flexibility			
Resistance to Common Illness			
Sexual Function			
Sexual Potency/Frequency			
Duration of Penile Erection			
Frequency of Nighttime Urination			
Hot Flashes & Related Symptoms			
Menstrual Cycle Regulation			
Mental Function			
Quality of Sleep			
Mental Energy & Clarity			
Emotional Stability			
Attitude Toward Life			
Memory			
TOTAL ALL AREAS			

For a current listing of Distributors and Clinicians who use Symbiotropin Therapy, contact:

Nutraceutics Corp. USA
3229 Morgan Ford Road
St. Louis MO 63116

(877) 664-6684 FAX (314) 664-4639

E-mail: info@nutraceutics.com
Web site: www.nutraceutics.com

MANUFACTURERS OF hGH INJECTIONS:

Eli Lilly .... Indianapolis, IN 800-545-5979
Ferring .... Suffern, NY 800-445-3690
Genentech .... San Francisco, CA 800-821-8590
Novo Nordisk .... Princeton, NJ 609-987-5800
Serano Labs .... Norwell, MA 617-982-9000

References available upon request.

The Effect of Symbiotropin® on Muscle Strength and Body Composition in Older Women

Yinka Thomas, MSc

Abstract

The effect of Symbiotropin® on muscle strength and body composition in older women. Aims: This investigation assessed the effects of a 12-week program of Symbiotropin® supplementation on muscle strength and body composition in older women. Studies into the effect of human growth hormone (hGH) on physical and physiological effects of the aging process, has led to a proliferation of dietary supplements claiming to reverse these effects.

Methods: Twenty-eight female participants, aged 45-67, were randomly assigned in a blind, randomized placebo-controlled design, to a supplement (S, N=14), or placebo group (P, N=14). The S group took one Symbiotropin® tablet, dissolved in water, every night for 12 weeks. The P group took one identical-looking glucose tablet, also dissolved in water, every night. Measurements of muscle strength using a Cybex II isokinetic dynamometer, and body composition using waist circumference and skinfolds to calculate percentage body fat were made pre-study, at six weeks and on completion of the study. Participants were asked not to make any major dietary or physical activity alterations.

Results: Paired samples t-tests indicated significant increases in muscle strength and decreases in waist circumference and percentage body fat occurred in the S group ($p<0.05$), and also a significant decrease in percentage body fat in the P group ($p<0.05$). A t-test for equality of means produced significant differences in only percentage body fat between the two groups.

Conclusions: These findings indicate that Symbiotropin® supplementation can increase muscle strength and decrease percentage body fat, without any dietary or physical activity modification. Long-term studies are needed to test effectiveness and safety over longer periods, and other variables such as aerobic capacity. Key words: HUMAN GROWTH HORMONE SECRETAGOGUE, AGING, SUPPLEMENTATION, PERCENTAGE BODY FAT, MUSCLE PERFORMANCE.

The United Kingdom, along with other Western nations, has an aging population. The 2001 national census showed that for the first time there are now more people over 60 than there are children under 16 (10). This aging of the population reflects longer life expectancy, the fact that there have not been any events with a corresponding effect on life expectancy like that of the first and second world wars, and the fact that the 'baby boomers', those born between 1946 and 1964 are now reaching 'middle age'. This situation also presents major socio-economic implications because living longer does not necessarily mean living well, and the State faces the possibility of having to care for a large population of older adults who may be unable to care for themselves. This has led to increased scientific interest in the aging process of the human body, and aging is now seen by many as a disease rather than an inevitable consequence of getting older, primarily because it is progressive and degenerative, it affects every cell, tissue, and organ of the body, and ultimately ends in death. Although there are well documented methods of slowing the aging process by physical activity (54), nutrition (55), under-nutrition (9, 27), and vitamin and mineral supplementation (59), it has until recently been thought of as irreversible. However modern science is now developing methods of actually halting and reversing the aging process. Some of these methods, such as stem cell research and gene therapy, are very recent discoveries and inaccessible to most of the population. However hormone therapy involving human growth hormone somatotropin (hGH) and growth hormone (GH) secretagogues like Symbiotropin®, are now well-established products that claim to reverse the aging process, are available in tablet form, classed as food supplements not drugs, and are readily available.

Changes in body composition in older adults, particularly the increase of percentage body fat (%BF) and sarcopenia are well documented (8, 22, 44, 45, 57), and a definitive consequence of skeletal muscle atrophy with aging is the reduction in muscle strength. Muscle strength appears to be relatively well maintained until 50 years of age. Thereafter, a 15% loss in muscle strength per decade occurs between 50 and 70 years (43), with a 30% loss in muscle strength in the years between 70 and 80 (16). This change in body composition and decrease in skeletal muscle strength appears to be a factor in the onset of age-related diseases that lead to disability and infirmity including coronary heart disease, atherosclerosis, cerebrovascular disease, diabetes, obesity, osteoporosis, and osteoarthritis. Rudman (1985) found that between the ages of thirty and seventy-five, adipose tissue on average expands by 100% and bone mass declines by an average of 20%. Therefore, because of their implications in the age-related diseases outlined, obesity management and the preservation of quality lean tissue are integral to maintaining function and quality of life in older adults, and these factors form the basis of anti-aging research involving hGH.

It was around fifty years ago that it was first proposed that aging and the diseases of aging have their origin in, and are controlled by the hypothalamus/pituitary complex located at the base of the brain. This hypothesis was termed "The Neuroendocrine Theory of Aging and Degenerative Disease," and two conclusions from this theory were that it is impossible to retard the development of the main degenerative diseases without retarding the rate of normal aging, and the main mechanisms of aging and degenerative disease are reversible phenomena. hGH is actually a small protein molecule that contains 191 amino acids in a single polypeptide chain, and is fundamentally implicated in the aging process of the human body. It is the most common hormone secreted by the anterior pituitary gland, and its rate of production peaks during adolescence when accelerated growth occurs. The hypothalamus is the central control center that regulates the secretion of somatotropin from the pituitary. The usual release of hGH in the brain depends on the interplay between a hormone that promotes hGH release, growth hormone-releasing hormone (GHRH), and one that inhibits it called somatostatin. GHRH stimulates the production and release of hGH from the anterior pituitary somatotrophs, assisted by the GH secretagogue (GHS) ghrelin (50, 62, 83). Somatostatin inhibits the secretion, but not the synthesis of hGH, and it is more effective in inhibiting hGH stimulated by GHRH than hGH stimulated by the GHS ghrelin (60). GH is released in pulses that take place during the day and night, with its release being especially prominent during the early phases of sleep. These pulses of hGH secretion are converted in the liver within just 20 minutes to Insulin-like Growth Factor Type I (IGF-1). Although IGF-1 is not insulin, it acts like insulin as it promotes glucose transfer through cell membranes into the cell, and it elicits most of the effects associated with hGH. It is measured in the blood and is the surrogate marker of growth hormone in the body.

Due to mechanisms not fully understood, the amount of growth hormone secreted into the body starts to decline after peaking during late adolescence (79, 80). At the age of twenty-one the measurable level of hGH in the body is 10 mg per deciliter of blood, and at sixty-one the level is 2 mg per deciliter of blood – a decrease of 80 per cent. This reduced level of secretion, referred to as somatopause, coincides with the process of aging that the body undergoes over a period of time which results in reduced muscle mass, increased body fat, thinning and wrinkling of skin, thinning and greying of hair, reduced energy, reduced muscle strength, decreased libido, less restful sleep and other physiological changes. More specifically, between ages thirty and seventy-five years, there is a 20-50% reduction in the size of muscle, liver, kidney and spleen. The reduction in lean body mass has been shown to reflect atrophic processes in skeletal muscle, liver, kidney, spleen, skin and bone (63).

The landmark studies that established the link between hGH and aging were conducted in the 1990s and showed that age reversal was possible with the use of hGH (63). Further studies have shown the effect of hGH therapy on body composition (1, 2, 3, 4, 12, 13, 14, 17, 18, 23, 38, 39, 53, 77), and skeletal muscle strength (33, 37, 38, 39, 64, 65). GH replacement therapy has also shown beneficial normalizing effects on parameters such as cardiac and renal function, thyroid hormone metabolism, bone metabolism, sweat secretion, total and regional fuel metabolism and psychological well being (2, 3, 35, 47, 52). Rudman et al (1990) studied adult men aged between 61 and 73 years who had measured deficiencies in hGH. They were injected with GH produced from recombinant DNA synthesis initially for a period of six months, and results showed an increase in lean body mass of 8.8%, and decrease in fat mass of 14.4%, an increase in bone density of 1.6%, and an increase in skin thickness of 7.1%. The participants did not exercise. These effects of human growth hormone on lean body mass and adipose-tissue mass were equivalent to 10 to 20 years of reversed aging. The decrease in fat-mass is particularly significant in aging because the increase in fatty tissue is related to a variety of cardiovascular problems, while the loss of lean body mass is linked to older adults losing energy, strength, and mobility. Any factor that can slow or reverse the trend towards more fatty tissue will, in effect, slow or reverse the aging process itself. As well as the physiological benefits of hGH therapy observed in studies and already outlined, growth hormone deficiency is also synonymous with various physical and physiological complaints that collectively influence quality of life (QoL), including mood fluctuations, disturbed sleeping patterns, low libido, and low energy levels (47).

One key characteristic of hGH is that it is an anabolic hormone as opposed to a catabolic hormone such as the stress hormones. Thus, the age-reversing results of Rudman's and other studies were achieved because of hGH's regenerative properties on tissues throughout the body. hGH plays a key role in the aging process partly because it improves utilization of fat as a source of energy by stimulating lipolysis and fat oxidation. All fat cells have hGH receptors, and when it binds to these receptors, it triggers a series of enzymatic reactions in the cells to break down fat, making it available as fuel and reducing the size of fat cells. Studies have also shown that cortisol and insulin facilitate lipid accumulation by expressing lipoprotein lipase (LPL). hGH and testosterone inhibit the expression of LPL, which markedly stimulates lipolysis (33). hGH increases lean body mass through stimulation of protein synthesis, and reduction of protein oxidation, without inhibiting protein catabolism (39). Another characteristic of the aging process is weight-gain, and this can partly be attributed to long term IGF-1 deficiency, as seen in older adults, slowing carbohydrate metabolism, leading to insulin resistance and often weight gain. These effects can be reversed with hGH, which increases glucose turnover (39). All of these factors can be attributable to the results of Rudman's studies.

When Rudman extended his study into a seventh month, several participants developed debilitating carpal tunnel syndrome, and others developed severe arthritis, high blood pressure, congestive heart disease, and diabetic-like conditions. Although the side effects diminished when the drug was discontinued, so did the benefits. This study led to further research into hGH in an attempt to gain the benefits and avoid the harmful side effects. These further studies investigated the body's mechanisms for producing hGH. It had been thought that the production of hGH in the body naturally decreased as an individual got older, however the production of the hormone does not decline with age, but the body continues to produce hGH well into old age. What actually declines is the body's efficiency in releasing the hGH that it is still producing. Due to reasons not yet discovered, hGH remains sequestered in pituitary somatotrophs, rather than being secreted into the body. It has already been established that specific hGH releasing peptides called GHS's were identified to be instrumental in enhancing the body's production, release and utilization of IGF-1 (56). GHS's are a natural polyamino acid chain that are postulated to initiate the pituitary gland to release growth hormone. While hGH causes the body to act as if the pituitary has released growth hormone, GHS's actually cause the release of it. Hence a secretagogue causes the bodies own natural processes to produce growth hormone. The GHS Ghrelin was only recently discovered in 1999 by Kojima et al (41), and the true physiological importance of GHS's is now just being discovered by further research (15, 67). The secretagogue Symbiotropin® being tested in this study is based on the discovery in 1981 of peptides that are similar in structure to naturally occurring pain substances such as enkaphalin in the human brain. Enkaphalin acts like a natural form of morphine in ameliorating pain perception, and for some unknown reason, also stimulates GH release.

As already mentioned, GHS's act independently of the inhibitory hGH substance somatostatin, making them of extreme interest to researchers because they appear to increase the active anabolic derivative of hGH, IGF-1, and therefore they have a potential benefit in treating many catabolic diseases. The advantage of these peptides is that they are available orally, unlike hGH or IGF-1, which must be administered only by injection. Synthetic GHS's have been developed, which include GH-releasing peptide (GHRP), a synthetic hexapeptide, which has been demonstrated to be a potent, relatively selective GHS in humans (7, 29). Other compounds have been developed that mimic the stimulatory actions of GHRP on GH release in animals and man (26, 71). Further research studied the effects of oral treatment with the GHS MK-677 on GH secretion and body composition in otherwise healthy obese males (75). This study was randomized, double blind, parallel, and placebo controlled. Twenty-four obese males, aged 18–50 years, with body mass indexes greater than 30 kg/m2 and waist/hip ratios greater than 0.95, were treated with MK-677 25 mg (n = 12) or placebo (n = 12) daily for 8 weeks. Results reported IGF-1 increased by approximately 40% with MK-677 treatment, and serum IGF-binding protein-3 was also significantly increased. GH was significantly increased after the initial dose of MK-677, and these increases persisted at 2 and 8 weeks of treatment. Fat-free mass increased significantly in the MK-677 treatment group when determined with dual energy x-ray absorptiometry. However, total and visceral fat were not significantly changed with active therapy. The researchers concluded that 8 weeks treatment with MK-677 in healthy obese males caused a sustained increase in serum levels of GH, IGF-I, and IGF-binding protein-3, and changes in body composition and energy expenditure were of an anabolic nature, with a sustained increase in fat-free mass and a transient increase in basal metabolic rate. They did not measure changes in body fat.

Similar to Svensson et al, Chapman et al (11) investigated the effect of the hGH releasing peptide MK-677 on the GH/IGF1 axis in selected growth hormone deficient adults. Nine severely hGH-deficient men who had been treated for their deficiency with growth hormone injections during childhood were studied. In a double-blind, rising-dose design, subjects received once daily oral doses of 10 or 50 mg MK-677, or placebo for 4 days over two treatment periods separated by at least 28 days. Results showed that serum IGF-1 and GH concentrations increased in all subjects after treatment with both 10 and 50 mg/day MK-677. These key studies support the hypothesis that the synthetic secretagogue MK-677 increases serum levels of GH, IGF-1, and IGF-binding protein-3, produces a sustained increase in fat-free mass and a transient increase in basal metabolic rate. GHS's were seen as preferred alternatives to hGH injections because they not only eliminated the need for injections, but they produced similar benefits, but without the harmful side effects.

It was based on the findings of studies with drug versions of oral GHS's, that a natural supplement form. Symbiotropin®, was developed. The primary ingredient in the supplement is pituitary peptides, similar in structure to the drug versions, together with what the developers call 'chaperone molecules', which enhance both the effectiveness and delivery of the supplement in the body. Symbiotropin® also contains several known GH-releasing amino acids, such as arginine, glutamine, GABA, glycine, lysine and tyrosine, that are delivered into tissues and not broken down beforehand by the chaperone molecules. The supplement also contains a legume found in the tropical rain forest called Lacuna bean that is naturally high in L-dopa, which is a known GH releaser.

Symbiotropin® has been investigated in a study evaluating 36 individuals with low levels of IGF-1 for changes in serum igf-1 levels and other noticeable changes, over a period of 12 weeks (31). Participants experienced a 30% average increase in IGF-1. The researchers also noted positive participant self-assessments in areas of endurance and body composition, hair and skin condition, sexual function, wound healing, immune function, and mental function, and noted significant improvements in all areas ranging from 21-71%. However, although these results were telling, participant self-assessment is not as reliable as clinical observation of these physical and mental changes. The clinical observations that the researchers made in this study showed significant improvements in blood sugar management in diabetic participants, lowered prostate specific antigen, improved cardiac and pulmonary function, improved blood pressure management, and improvement in menopausal symptoms, though they give no indication of how these observations were measured.

The aim of this study was to investigate the effect of GHS Symbiotropin® percentage body fat, and muscle strength in the study group of women aged 45-70. It used validated methods of body composition assessment and muscle strength evaluation, to test the effectiveness of the supplement which is widely sold as an 'anti-aging' supplement. Aging is associated with reduced GH, IGF-1, increased body fat particularly abdominal fat, and decreased lean body mass and muscle strength, as well as other physical changes that will not be measured in this study, though participant self-assessments will be noted. It is hypothesized that the GHS Symbiotropin® will cause an increase in muscle strength, and a decrease in percentage body fat in women aged 45-70 years.

Materials and Methods

This study was approved by the St Mary's College Ethics Committee, (see Appendix 1). All participants gave written informed consent (see Appendix 2). A randomized, controlled, masked placebo design was used to study the effects of 12 weeks of oral administration of the GHS Symbiotropin®. Twenty-eight females between 45-67 years were randomly recruited using advertisements in local newspapers and a university notice board. Twenty-five of the participants were white, and three were of African origin. Respondees were sent an information pack about the study (see Appendix 3), and the final 28 subjects were randomly placed, depending on the order they arrived at the testing center, into the study group to receive Symbiotropin®, or the control group to receive a matching dose of placebo daily for 12 weeks (n = 14 per group). The Symbiotropin® dose was administered by the participants themselves, and consisted of one tablet dissolved in a 250ml glass of water, and taken every night before retiring. The placebo used was an effervescent glucose tablet produced by the manufacturers of Symbiotropin®. Participants were asked to inform their general practitioner that they were taking part in this study if they were under medical supervision for any condition. The placebo group was offered the supplement after completion of the study, and the participants were not instructed with any new information about changing their nutritional habits or physical activity (PA) routines, but asked not to change their ordinary daily calorific intake or physical activity during the course of the study.

Before the start of the study, participants' weight in kilograms, waist circumference in centimeters, percentage body fat, and muscle strength were measured. Waist circumference was measured in the standing position with a flexible plastic tape placed around the navel. Waist circumference was used rather than waist to hip ratio, as waist size gives a better indicator of visceral fat proportions (19, 81). Measures for percentage body fat were calculated using skinfold (SKF) measurements taken by Harpenden Callipers. In order that measures were consistently taken from the same sites on the body, guidelines for their anatomical location were adhered to (28). Measures were taken from the middle of the triceps muscle using a vertical fold; the biceps, again using a vertical fold and in the middle of the muscle; the subscapular, using a diagonal fold and just below the angle of scapular; and suprailiac, just above the suprailiac crest. Three readings in rotation were taken for each measurement. Percentage body fat from SKF was calculated using the Durnin & Wormersley equation (21).

All subjects were tested for both knee extension and flexion strength in the right leg with the Cybex II isokinetic dynamometer. Isokinetic tests were measured at 60°. Average torque values were collected throughout the range of motion in Newton-meters relative to body weight. The test involved the subject sitting in an upright position with the hips flexed to 90 degrees. Pelvic and thigh straps were used to stabilize the hips and thighs. The axis of rotation of the knee joint was identified, and the input shaft of the dynamometer was aligned with the axis of rotation of the knee joint. The length of the lever arm was adjusted so that the participant's shin contacted the shin pad above the ankle, and the ankle strap was secured when the knee was at full flexion. The participant held the side handles of the machine, or they could fold their arms across the chest (the position was kept constant throughout every test).

The leg movements were explained and demonstrated, and the subject first warmed up by making 5 sub-maximal repetitions. After a rest of about 5 minutes, the participant performed the test. The speed was set at 60 degrees, the lowest speed. Maximal strength was measured by performing three repetitions, resting for a period of 3-5 minutes between each one. Muscle strength was measured by peak isokinetic torque. The participants were asked to indicate if they felt undue discomfort or pain, and the test was halted. The highest scores for flexion and extension of each leg were noted, and finally the participants were taken through a series of stretches of the quadriceps and hamstrings after the testing session. All measurements were taken before commencing the study, at six weeks, and on completion of the study at 12 weeks.

Results were statistically analyzed using SPSS. Descriptive statistics for the dependent variables were computed to determine mean and standard deviation values. T-tests for independent samples were used to assess the between group differences, and within-group differences were analyzed using a series of T-tests for related samples.

In addition to the measured data, because growth hormone deficiency in older adults is also associated with physical and psychological changes that affect QoL, participants were also asked to make a note of and report any other changes that they experienced during the course of the study. They were not instructed on any changes to look out for, and despite the existence of a QoL Assessment of Growth Hormone Deficiency in Adults Questionnaire that has been shown to have good reliability and construct validity (20, 48), they were not given this because these QoL variables were not being tested. They were simply asked to report any changes that they felt.

Results

Twenty-eight participants were initially recruited to take part in this study, however due to compliance failure with the testing schedule, only 10 participants completed the study from the placebo (P) group, and 12 participants completed from the study (S) group. The average age of the participants was 54.6 years ($\pm$6.9) years (see table 1), and there were no significant differences (p>0.05) between the two groups with regard to body weight at the beginning of the study. Participants, weight percentage body fat (%BF), waist circumference, and isokinetic muscle strength were recorded at the beginning of the study, then all of the variables except for body mass (which was not a tested variable), were measured half-way through the trial at six weeks, then on completion at twelve weeks. The descriptive statistics are presented as the mean and standard deviation of all of the variables: waist circumference, sum of skin-folds, percentage body fat, and muscle strength.

Paired samples t-tests indicated significant decreases in percentage body fat (%BF) and waist circumference in the study (S) group (p<0.05), and significant increases in muscle strength for both flexors and extensors in the study group (p<0.05) at 12 weeks. Also in the S group, the six-weeks data indicated a significant decrease in percentage body fat (%BF) (p<0.05), and significant increases in muscle strength for both flexors and extensors (p<0.05), but no significant decrease in waist circumference (p>0.05). In the placebo (P) group, a paired samples t-tests indicated that the only variable that produced a significant result was for %BF at 12-weeks (p<0.05). All other data at both 6 and 12 weeks produced no significant changes (p>0.05). For waist circumference, the average decrease was 1.8%, and the largest decrease 6.7% in the S group (see table 2). A t-test for equality of means produced significant differences in only percentage body fat data collected at 12 weeks between the two groups, due to them both producing significant results for this variable. However the average decrease in %BF in the P group was 4%, and in the S group over double that figure at 8.9% (see table 3, page 11).

For isokinetic muscle strength, paired samples t-tests indicated significant increases in the S group only (p<0.05). For the flexors, the largest increase was 600%, and for the extensors, and the largest increase was 244%, (from the same participant). These results were due to the participant, who suffers from arthritis of the spine, registering very little

Table 1. Age and weight of study participants

Participant P group	Age (yrs)	Weight (kg)	Participant S group	Age (yrs)	Weight (kg)
1	58	73	1	50	68
2	56	64	2	54	77
3	57	62	3	64	62
4	63	50	4	45	64
5	45	74	5	50	64
6	64	81	6	64	70
7	64	66	7	49	61
8	48	99	8	50	70
9	46	65	9	58	66
10	61	72	10	46	68
11	56	75	11	53	87
12	47	62	12	63	65
13	50	94	13	67	65
14	50	60	14	51	88
Mean	54.6	71.2	Mean	54.5	69.6
Standard deviation	6.9	13.2	Standard deviation	7.2	8.5

muscle strength at the commencement of the study and showing gains in strength during the course of the trial. However because of these large increases, her results were excluded from the final data analysis.

The overall increase in peak torque at 12 weeks was 8.7% in the P group, and 25.85% in the S group. Figure 1 shows the mean percentage difference between the pre and post intervention measures for all four variables at 6 weeks, and Figure 2 shows the mean percentage differences at 12 weeks.

Table 2 (see page 10) shows the results for waist circumference after 12 weeks. Data indicates a mean percentage increase of 0.08 for the placebo group, and a significant decrease of -1.8% for the study group ($p<0.05$).

Table 3 (see page 11) shows the results for %BF after 12 weeks, indicating significant mean percentage decreases of -4.9% in placebo group and -9.6 in study group.

Table 2. Waist circumference results at 12 weeks

P group participant	Waist pre (cm)	Waist post (cm)	% difference	S group participant	Waist pre (cm)	Waist post (cm)	% difference
1	89	88	-1.12	1	89	94	5.6
2	79	--	--	2	104	101	-2.9
3	79	75	-5	3	80	--	--
4	68.5	68	-0.7	4	79	75	-5
5	76	80	-5.2	5	81.5	81	-0.6
6	105	--	--	6	104	100	3.8
7	89	89	0	7	79	79	0
8	118	118	0	8	84	78	-7.1
9	80	80	0	9	83	--	--
10	82	84	2.4	10	86	83	-3.5
11	101	--	--	11	103	96	-6.7
12	87	87	0	12	92	89	-3.2
13	94	94	0	13	82	82	0
14	71	--	--	14	104	102	-2
Mean	86.25	86.3	0.08		90.62	88.33	-1.8
SD	13.39	13.42			10.39	9.85	

Tables 4 and 5 (see pages 12 and 13) show results of changes in isokinetic muscle strength after 12 weeks of intervention. The mean percentage increases of 17.1% for flexors and 15.5% for extensors in the placebo group were not significant, and the mean percentage increases of 79.7% and 35.70% for flexors and extensors in the study group were significant changes.

Figure 1 (see page 14) shows the mean percentage differences between pre and post measures for all variables at 12 weeks

There was also evidence of other positive subjective responses from the participants in the study group, the most common response being increased energy levels felt during the first four weeks by many of the participants (see Appendix 4). Other responses included feeling that arms had become leaner, more restful sleep, and increased libido. All of the participants in the study group felt one or more positive change except for one who suffered a bereavement during the course of the study, and another who was on anti-depressants. They both expressed that their minds were on things other than the study.

Table 3. Percentage body fat results at 12 weeks

P group participant	%BF pre	%BF post	% difference	S group participant	%BF pre	%BF post	% difference
1	38.8	34.3	-11.5	1	38	38.4	1
2	31.2	--	--	2	47	39.8	-15.3
3	35.5	32	-9.8	3	33.5	--	--
4	30	29	-3.3	4	40.8	36.2	-11.2
5	38.4	35.5	-7.5	5	39	33	-15.3
6	40.8	--	--	6	45.6	40.3	-11.6
7	37.2	36.7	-1.3	7	34.7	32.5	-6.3
8	48	47.9	-.2	8	37	35.1	-5.1
9	33.7	31.3	-7.1	9	35.2	--	--
10	35.6	35.6	0.0	10	32	29.1	-9
11	43.1	--	--	11	41.8	39.5	-5.5
12	35.2	32.5	-7.6	12	35	29	-17.1
13	38.4	37.9	-1.3	13	41.1	37.6	-8.5
14	32.6	--	--	14	45	39.8	-11.5
Mean	37.08	35.27	-4.9		39.75	35.85	-9.6
SD	4.66	5.19			4.67	4.11	

No side effects were observed during the trial in any of the participants.

Discussion

The purpose of this study was to test whether the GHS Symbiotropin® can decrease percentage body fat, and increase muscle strength in the study group of women aged 45-67. This specific group was chosen because the declining functional capacity of older adults is a major concern, and the loss of muscle mass and strength is a prime cause. The data collected indicates that Symbiotropin® can significantly increase isokinetic muscle strength in both flexors and extensors, and decrease waist circumference and percentage body fat over a period of twelve weeks.

These findings are consistent with numerous other studies involving hGH administration and body composition (1, 2, 3, 4, 12, 13, 14, 17, 18, 23, 38, 39, 53, 63, 77), and studies involving hGH and muscle strength (33, 37, 38, 39, 64, 65). This is the first study testing the effect of Symbiotropin® on body composition and muscle strength. The mecha-

Table 4. Isokinetic muscular performance - Flexors at 12 weeks

P group participant	Peak torque pre	Peak torque post	% difference	S group participant	Peak torque pre	Peak torque post	% difference
1	33	38	15	1	43	35	-18.6
2	43	--	--	2	5	35	600
3	41	42	2.4	3	11	--	--
4	26	46	77	4	20	47	135
5	73	62	15	5	27	45	66
6	31	--	--	6	27	22	-18
7	53	46	-13.2	7	56	61	9
8	69	39	-43.5	8	41	52	26.8
9	50	66	32	9	47	--	--
10	33	52	57.5	10	69	83	20.2
11	60	--	--	11	37	49	32.4
12	60	62	3.3	12	39	50	28.2
13	42	53	26	13	39	53	36
14	49	--	--	14	43	60	39.5
Mean	48	50.6	17.1		36.3	50.63	32.4
SD	15.83	10.07			16.49	15.33	

nisms by which Symbiotropin® exerts its effects on muscle and fat tissue to produce the results of this study may be ascribed to the anabolic and lipolytic effects of GH. Symbiotropin® as a GHS, resists the effects of the GH inhibitor somatostatin, helping to increase the body's release of hGH. This in turn may have improved the utilization of fat as a source of energy and inhibits the expression of LPL stimulating lipolysis (33), which may account for the decrease in %BF. Increased levels of hGH in the body also increases lean mass by stimulating protein catabolism (39), which may account for the increase in isokinetic muscle strength.

The significant decrease in %BF in the P group may be accounted for by a combination of the 'placebo effect', whereby a psychological belief in the treatment and a subjective feeling of improvement leads to a change in dietary and PA behavior eliciting a positive response. The timing of the study may also be a factor, as the study commenced soon after the New Year, participants may have lost weight due to resuming normal nutritional

Table 5. Isokinetic muscular performance - Extensors at 12 weeks

P group participant	Peak torque pre	Peak torque post	% difference	S group participant	Peak torque pre	Peak torque post	% difference
1	52	58	11.5	1	80	61	-23
2	56	--	--	2	9	31	244
3	60	64	6.7	3	14	--	--
4	37	54	46	4	54	53	-1.8
5	102	106	4	5	47	58	23.4
6	48	--	--	6	43	37	-14
7	79	83	5	7	94	103	9.5
8	79	50	-36.7	8	73	88	20.5
9	50	94	88	9	47	--	--
10	56	69	23.2	10	89	121	36
11	83	--	--	11	46	77	67.3
12	94	91	3.2	12	49	65	32.6
13	47	45	4.2	13	58	69	19
14	65	--	--	14	89	103	15.7
Mean	65.6	71.4	15.5		60.91	72.16	19.3
SD	21.61	20.88			24.88	27.37	

habits after a season usually associated with an increase in calorific consumption. This is supported by the fact that in the P group, there was no significant increase in muscle strength, which can only be produced by hGH or GHS therapy as this and other mentioned studies show, and resistance training (RT).

The results of this study are noteworthy because the consequences of sarcopenia, a muscle wasting disease, can be extensive. Individuals are more susceptible to falls and fractures, impaired in ability to regulate body temperature, slower in metabolism, and may suffer an overall loss in the ability to perform everyday tasks (32). Muscle atrophy appears to result from a gradual loss of both muscle fiber size and number. A gradual loss in muscle cross-sectional area is consistently found with advancing age; by age 50, about ten percent of muscle area is gone. After 50 years of age, the rate accelerates significantly. Muscle strength declines by approximately 15 percent per decade in the sixties and seventies and by about 30 percent thereafter. Although intrinsic muscle function is reduced

Mean percentage differences

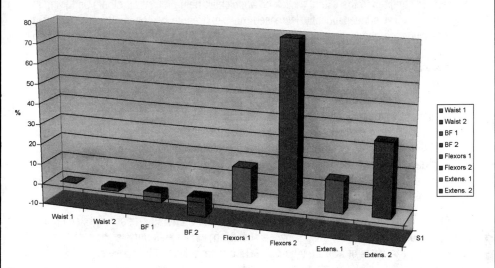

with advancing age, age-related decrease in muscle mass is responsible for almost all loss of strength in the older adult. The number of functional motor units also declines with advancing age, which requires surviving motor units to innervate a greater number of muscle fibers. Inactivity has been shown to play a role in loss of muscle mass and strength, and RT is the key intervention to counter this and maintain or increase lean body mass, particularly the type II fast muscle fibers associated with strength and power that atrophy more quickly. Among women over 50, 83% do not participate in enough PA to benefit their health (70). Because adherence to an PA routine is generally low in most population groups and especially older adults (70), the alternative of taking a dietary supplement that can produce an increase in muscle strength, and reduce %BF without having to exercise would be fundamentally attractive to many individuals.

Aging and functional decline is now being taken so seriously that the United States National Institutes of Health have funded a seven year longitudinal study, targeted toward understanding the functional decline of healthier older adults by focusing on older adults in transition from good health to frailty. The Health, Aging, and Body Composition Study (HEALTH ABC) cohort consists of 3,075 black and white men and women aged 70-79, and results so far have found that lower strength with older age was predominantly due to a lower muscle mass. Age and body fat also had significant inverse associations with strength and muscle quality. The researchers concluded that both preservation of lean mass and prevention of gain in fat may be important in maintaining strength and muscle quality in old age (51). The HEALTH ABC study also founds that among older adults, higher levels of visceral fat are associated with greater aortic stiffness (73), and higher levels of fat tissue increases risk of developing type 2 diabetes (25). These studies demonstrate the links between increased body fat and decreased muscle strength with serious illness, functional capacity and quality of life in older adults.

Improved muscle strength can make the difference between an older adult being on their feet, or confined to the use of a stick or wheelchair, being reliant on others and living in a home or living independently. Increased muscle strength has been shown to maintain independence and well-being (84), improve balance and coordination (72), and reduce risk of falls (68). A fall can have a devastating effect on an individual's independence, confidence and quality of life, often leading to a spiral of inactivity and further decline (76). The loss of muscle power in older adults at the rate of 30% per decade (69), is most pronounced in women (30), therefore improving muscle strength is a particular concern for women. In women over 50, 28% do not have the strength and power in their leg muscles to be able to climb the stairs easily, compared with 7% of men, and in women aged 70-74 this figure rises to 47% (70). The decrease in strength in women over 50 is greater than decreases in aerobic capacity and flexibility (70). Studies show that these figures can be drastically reduced by an increase in skeletal muscle strength, which results show can be achieved by treating growth hormone deficiency (GHD) with GH therapy.

GHD in adults is associated with reduced muscle mass and muscle strength, and previous studies involving hGH also shown a significant increase in muscle strength. A study involving two years of hGH treatment in GH-deficient adults (33), increased and normalized isokinetic and isometric muscle strength. The GH-deficient subjects had lower isometric knee extensor, knee flexor, and hand-grip strength than the reference population. hGH treatment produced significant results in isometric knee extensor and flexor strengths. The increase in muscle strength was more marked in younger patients and in patients with lower initial muscle strength than predicted. Another study showed that participants who had been on GH therapy for a year, showed significantly increased isometric strength in the quadriceps muscle when compared with those who had been taking the therapy for four months or had taken a placebo (37), and other studies show similar results of GH treatment increasing muscle strength and mass (38, 39, 64, 65). These studies differ fundamentally in that the participants were GH deficient adults. This study chose participants randomly who were not known, or tested to show profound GHD, yet the results were, as in earlier studies, still significant.

Before hGH research, resistance training was the established and effective method of combating sarcopenia by increasing muscle mass and strength, and studies involving older adults had produced significant increases in both strength and muscle mass. One study involved 39 women with a mean age of 59, who were placed in a control group or strength training group that trained twice weekly for twelve months (49). In the study group, the one repetition max was increased by 74% (lattissimus dorsi pull-down), 35% (knee extensor), and 75% (leg press). The control group showed increases of 13%, 3.7%, and 18% respectively. Most strength gains in the study group occurred within the first twelve weeks of the study. Other studies have shown that older individuals can increase and maintain muscle mass with resistance training. One study showed that 70 year old men who had resistance trained since 50 years, had muscle cross-sectional area and strength comparable to a group of 28-year-old sedentary subjects (40). In another study, a group of 90-year-old individuals had a mean area enlargement of 12% in trained muscles after eight weeks of resistance training (24). These studies demonstrate that similar gains in muscle strength that were achieved in this study can be obtained from a program of progressive resistance training, although, once again the potential problem of adherence to a physical activity program has to be overcome.

Although there is a strong body of research supporting the role of GH as a means of increasing muscle strength or mass, research does exist that does not support a role for GH, either alone or combined with RT, as a means of increasing muscle strength in healthy male older adults (42). This study involved 31 men (age, 74 ± 1 yr), who were assigned to either RT group and placebo (n = 8), RT + GH (n = 8), GH (n = 8), or placebo (n = 7). Measurements of isokinetic quadriceps muscle strength, quadriceps muscle power, quadriceps muscle fiber type, size, and myosin heavy chain (MHC) composition; quadriceps cross-sectional area (CSA), body composition (dual-energy x-ray absorptiometry scanning), and GH-related serum markers were performed at baseline and after 12 weeks. Results found that GH alone had no effect on isokinetic quadriceps muscle strength, power, CSA, or fibre size. However, a substantial increase in MHC 2X isoform was observed with GH administration alone, and this may be regarded as a change into a more youthful MHC composition, possibly induced by the rejuvenating of systemic IGF-I levels. RT plus placebo caused substantial increases in quadriceps isokinetic strength, power, and CSA; but these RT induced improvements were not further augmented by additional GH administration. In the RT + GH group, there was a significant decrease in MHC 1 and 2X isoforms, whereas MHC 2A increased. RT, therefore, seemed to overrule the changes in MHC composition induced by GH administration alone. Changes in body composition confirmed previous reports of decreased fat mass, increased fat-free mass, and unchanged bone mineral content with GH administration, and worryingly, a high incidence of side effects were reported. It is difficult to account for these results, though it is possible that the GH used was inhibited by the actions of somatostatin, or the dosage may have been incorrect, especially as the participants experienced side-effects.

In conclusion, this data suggests that the GHS secretagogue Symbiotropin® is a viable alternative to hGH injections, and cardiovascular and RT in normalizing body composition and increasing muscle strength. Strength is a crucial component of quality of life. As life expectancy increases, the age-related decline in muscle strength becomes a matter of increasing importance. Maintenance of muscular strength significantly impacts an older person's ability to perform activities of daily living. In addition, maintaining and increasing strength to meet and exceed performance goals is important to a growing number of older adults who wish to live a fit, active lifestyle. In comparison to other studies involving hGH therapy and muscle strength, this study is notable in that it produced significant results after only twelve weeks, whereas some studies lasted two years (33). Also participants in this study took one tablet per dose, whilst two tablets per dose have been used in previous studies involving Symbiotropin® and is the recommended dose. Only one tablet was taken because that is the dosage that was approved by the Ethics Committee. The implications of hGH therapy are potentially enormous. According to research, all older adults are deficient in hGH (79), and other studies have shown that by age 70 to 80, 38% of the American adult population is as deficient in growth hormone as children who fail to grow normally because of a hormonal lack (63). If aging is, as this and other studies suggest, a pituitary deficiency disease, then GHS treatment, which is more readily available as a food supplement than hGH which requires costly injections, may bring back the higher GH levels of youth which are associated with peak body function. GH treatment is not just for those who are grossly deficient. In middle and late adulthood, all adults experience a series of progressive alterations in body composition, including a loss of lean body mass, an increase in fat tissues, and atrophy of skeletal muscle, liver, kidney, spleen, skin and bone. It is possible that GH replacement will in the future become as routine as steroid, thyroid hormone, and sex hormone replacement therapy in management of the hypo-pituitary adult. The major restriction to the widespread use of GH is cost, which makes the GHS's a more attractive option. The prospect of GH replacement becoming routine, however, does raise a number of issues. The most fundamental of these relates to the selection criteria of patients who may benefit from GH therapy, as these results have shown that it is not only the severely GHD adult that can benefit. Whether the next generation of older adults, the 'baby boom' generation should be advised and recommended to take a supplement that may intervene in the aging process, improve their quality of life, and may also extend their life-spans, or whether nature should be allowed to 'take it's course', is a topic that needs to be debated.

The results from this study, and the subjective changes also noted warrant further investigation and study into the therapeutic and anti-aging potential of Symbiotropin®. Further research could include a long-term study involving the safety and effectiveness of Symbiotropin® treatment to show that it is as safe as GH therapy. A review of long-term (two and three year) studies involving lower doses of hGH found no evidence to suggest that this therapy caused any unfavorable long-term side-effects (61). GHD in adults is associated with abnormal average body composition, characterized by an increase in adipose tissue mass and a decrease in muscle mass and isokinetic skeletal strength. These changes are the logical results of the metabolic abnormalities that characterize the GHD syndrome. Long-term GH replacement therapy normalizes body composition and increases muscle strength, and as the results of this study suggest, so does a 12 week course of the GHS Symbiotropin®. Other research could also include men, though the majority of the studies conducted into hGH and aging include male participants. And other variables could be tested, for example aerobic capacity. There were certain limitations involved in this study. A participant in the S group suffers from arthritis of the spine, and had very little strength at the initial testing stage, however made large improvements in strength during the course of the study. Her percentage differences of 600% for flexors and 244% for extensors may have had an effect on the results, though without her data, the mean increase in isokinetic muscle strength in the study group was still significant at 32.4% for flexors, and 16.8% for extensors. Improvements to the study design would include increasing the dosage of the supplement in the S group to two tablets per night, which is the recommended dosage by the manufacturers. This may have produced more profound results, or similar results but over a faster period of time. There was a high drop-out rate in this study (6 of the 28), and this may have been avoided if more participants had been chosen who lived close to the testing site, as a failure to attend the tests was a factor for the fall-out rate. There were also limitations regarding the reliability of the testing methods, in particular the percentage body fat measurements, because some of the participants were obese.

Caring for older adults is a major issue today with declining numbers of care homes, and insufficient pensions. This research adds to the increasing volume of studies that serve to enlighten the next generation of older adults the 40-60 year olds, increasing their awareness of the effects of aging, and highlighting the effectiveness of certain anti-aging methods to decrease the likelihood of their living dependent lifestyles when they reach older adulthood.

References

AL-SHOUMER, K.A.S., PAGE, B., THOMAS, E., MURPHY, M., BESHYAH, S.A. & JOHNSTON, D.G. Effects of four year's treatment with biosynthetic human growth hormone (GH) on body composition in GH deficient hypo-pituitary adults. European Journal of Endocrinology, 135, 559-67. 1996.

AMATO, G., CERELLA, C., FAZIO, S., LA MONTAGNA, G., CITTADINI, A., SABATINI, D., MARCIANO-MONE, C., SACCA, L. &BELLASTELLA, A. Body composition, bone metabolism and heart structure and function in growth hormone (GH)-deficient adults before and after GH replacement therapy at low doses. Journal of Clinical Endocrinology and Metabolism, 77, 1671-6. 1993.

BENGTSSON, B.A., EDEN, S, LONN, L et al. Treatment of Adults with Growth Hormone (GH) Deficiency with Recombinant Human GH. Journal of Clinical Endocrinology and Metabolism 76;309-317. 1993.

BINNERTS, A., DEURENBERG, P., SWART, G.R., WILSON, J.H.P. & LAMBERTS, S.W.J. Body composition in growth hormone-deficiency adults. Journal of Clinical Nature, 55, 918-23. 1992.

BINNERTS, A., SWART, G.R., WILSON, J.H.P., HOOGERBRUGGE, N., H.A.P., BIRKENHAGER, J.C. & LAMBERTS, S.W.J. . The effect of growth hormone administration in growth hormone deficient adults on bone, protein, carbohydrates and lipid homeostasis, as well as on body composition. Clinical Endocrinology, 37, 79-87.1992.

BOWERS C.Y., ALSTER D.K., FRENTZ J.M. The growth hormone-releasing activity of a synthetic hexapeptide in normal men and short statured children after oral administration. Journal of Clinical Endocrinology and Metabolism. 74:292–298. 1992.

BOWERS C.Y., REYNOLDS G.A., DURHAM D., BARRERA C.M., PEZZOLI S.S., THORNER M.O. Growth hormone (GH)-releasing peptide stimulates GH release in normal men and acts synergistically with GH-releasing hormone. Journal of Clinical Endocrinology and Metabolism. 70:975–982.1990.

BROOKS, S.V., AND FAULKNER, J.A. Age-associated weakness in skeletal muscles: underlying mechanisms. Medicine and Science in Sport and Exercise 26, 1994.

CALMAN, K., JACKSON, A.A. Nutritional aspects of the development of cancer. London: Stationery Office, 1998.

CENSUS 2001: National report for England and Wales, Office of National Statistics. 2001.

CHAPMAN I.A., PESCOVITZ O.H., MURPHY G, TREEP T, CERCHIO K.A., KRUPA D., GERTZB., POLVINO W.J., SKILES E.H., PEZZOLI S.S., THORNER M.O. Oral Administration of Growth Hormone (GH) Releasing Peptide-Mimetic MK-677 Stimulates the GH/Insulin-Like Growth Factor-I Axis in Selected GH-Deficient Adults. The Journal of Clinical Endocrinology and Metabolism . Vol. 82, No. 10 3455-3463. 1997.

COLLE, M. & AUZERIE, J. Discontinuation of growth hormone therapy in growth hormone deficient patients: assessment of body fat mass using bio-electric impedance. Hormone Research, 39, 1993.

CUNEO, R.C., JUDD, S., WALLACE, J.D., PERRY-KEENE, D., BURGER, H., LIM-TIO, S., STRAUSS, B., STOCKIGT, J., TOPLISS, D., ALFORD, F., HEW, L., BODE, H., CONWAY, A., HANDELSMAN, D., DUNN, S., BOYAGES, S., CHEUNG, N.W. & HURLEY, D. The Australian multicenter trial of growth hormone (GH) treatment in GH deficient adults. Journal of Clinical Endocrinology and Metabolism, 83, 107-16. 1998.

CUNEO, R.C., SALOMON, F., WILES, C.M., SONKSEN, P.H. Skeletal muscle performance in adults with growth hormone deficiency. Hormone Research, 33 (Suppl. 4), 55-60. 1990.

CUNHA, S.R., MAYO, K.E. Ghrelin and growth hormone secretagogues petentiate GH-releasing hormone induced cyclic adenosine 3', 5'-monophosphate production in cells expressing transfected GHRH and GH secretagogue receptors. Endocrinology Dec;143(12):4570-82. 2002.

DANNESKOLD-SAMSOE, B., KOFOD, V., MUNTER, J., GRIMBY, G., SCHOHR, P., AND JENSEN, G. Muscle strength and functional capacity in 78-81 year old men and women. European Journal of Applied Physiology. 52:310-314, 1984.

DE BOER, H., BLIK, G.J., VOERMAN, H.J., DE VRIES, P.M.J.M. & VAN DER VEEN, E.A. Body composition in adult growth hormone deficient men, assessed by anthropometry and bioimpedance analysis. Journal of Clinical Endocrinology and Metabolism, 75, 833-7. 1992.

DEGERBLAD, M., ELGINDY, N., HALL, K., SJOBERG, H.-E. & THOREN, M. Potent effect of recombinant growth hormone in bone mineral density and body composition in adults with panhypopituitarism. Acta Endocrinologica, 126, 387-93. 1992.

DESPRES, J.P. Lipoprotein metabolism in visceral obesity. International Journal of Obesity, 15, 45-52. 1991.

DOWARD, L.C. The development of the AGHDA: a measure to assess quality of life in childhood-onset and adult-onset GH deficiency. Quality of Life Research 4:420-421. 1995.

DURNIN, J.V., & WORMERSLEY, J. Body fat assessed from body density and its estimation from skinfold thickness: Measurements on 481 men and women aged from 16-72 years. British Journal of Nutrition, 32, 77-97. 1974.

FAULKNER, J.A., AND BROOKS, S.V. Age-related immobility: the roles of weakness, fatigue, injury and repair. Musculoskeletal Aging: Impact on Mobility. A.A. Buckwalter (Eds). American Academy of Orthopedic Surgeons 1993.

FELDMEIER, H.O., NASS, R.M., LANDGRAF, R. & STRASBURGER, D.J. Effects of growth hormone replacement therapy on glucose metabolism are due to changes of body composition. Journal of Pediatric Endocrinology and Metabolism, 10, 151-9. 1997.

FIATARONE, M.A., MARKS, E.C., RYAN, N.D., MEREDITH, L.A., LIPSITZ, A., AND EVANS, W.J. High-intensity training in nonagenarians. Journal of the American Medical Association. 263:3029-3034, 1990.

FRANSE, L.V., DI BARI, M., SHORR, R.I., RESNICK, H.E., VAN EIJK, J.T., BAUER, D.C., NEWMAN, A.B., AND PAHOR, M.; (Health, Aging, and Body Composition Study Group) Type 2 diabetes in older well-functioning people: who is undiagnosed? Data from the Health, Aging, and Body Composition study. Diabetes Care. Dec;24(12):2065-70. 2001.

GERTZ B.J., BARRETT J.S., EISENHANDLER R, et al. Growth hormone response in man to L-692,429, a novel nonpeptide mimic of growth hormone-releasing peptide-6. J Clin Endocronol Metab. 77:1393–1397. 1993.

GUARENTE, L., et al, Nature; 418:287-288, 344-348. 2002.

HARRISON, G.G., BUSKIRK, E.R., LINDSAY CARTER, J.E., JOHNSTON, F.E., LOHMAN, T.G., POLLOCK, M.L., ROCHE, A.F., & WILMORE, J.H. Skinfold thicknesses and measurement technique. In T.G. Lohman, A.F. Roche, & R. Martorell (Eds.), Anthropometric standardization reference manual (pp55-70). Champaign, Ill.: Human Kinetics. 1988.

ILSON B.E., JORKASKY D.K., CURNOW R.T., STOTE R.M. 1989 Effect of a new synthetic hexapeptide to selectively stimulate growth hormone release in healthy human subjects. J Clin Endocrenol Metab. 69:212–214.

IMAMURA, K., ASHIDA, A., ISHIKAWA, T. AND FUJII, M. Human major psoas muscle and sacrospinalis muscle in relation to age: a study by computed tomography. Journal of Gerontology. 38:678-681, 1983.

JAMIESON, J., DORMAN L. E. The role of somatotroph-specific peptides and IGF-1 intermediates as an alternative to HGH injections, presented at the American College for Advancement in Medicine, October 30, 1997.

JETTE, A.M., AND BRANCH, L.G. The Framingham disability study: II-Physical disability among the aging. American Journal of Public Health 71:1211-1216, 1981.

JOHANNSON, G., et al. Growth hormone treatment of abdominally obese men reduces abdominal fat mass, improves glucose and lipoprotein metabolism, and reduces diastolic blood pressure. Journal of Clinical Endocrinology and Metabolism; 82(3):727. 1997.

JOHANNSSON, G., GRIMBY, G., STIBRANT SUNNERHAGEN, K., AND BENGTSSON, B. Two Years of Growth Hormone (GH) Treatment Increase Isometric and Isokinetic Muscle Strength in GH-Deficient Adults. The Journal of Clinical Endocrinology and

Metabolism,Vol. 82, No. 9 2877-2884. 1997.

JOHNSTON DG, BENGTSSON BA. Workshop Report: the Effects of Growth Hormone and Growth Hormone Deficiency on Lipids and the Cardiovascular System. Acta Endocrinologica, 128 (Suppl 2): 69-70. 1993.

JORGENSEN, J.O.L., PEDERSON, S.A., THUESEN, L., JORGENSEN , J., INGEMANN-HANSEN, T., SKAKKEBEAK, N.E. & CHRISTIANSEN, J.S. Beneficial effects of growth hormone treatment in GH deficient adults. Lancet, 1, 1221-4. 1998.

JORGENSEN, J.O.L., PEDERSEN, S.A., THUESEN, L., JORGENSEN, J., MOLLER, J., MULLER, J., SKAKKEBEAK, N.E. & CHRISTIANSEN, J.S. Long-term growth hormone treatment in growth hormone deficient adults. Acta Endocrinologica, 125, 449-53. 1991.

JORGENSEN, J.O.L., THUESEN, L., MULLER, J., OVESEN, P., SKAKKEBAEK, N.E. & CHRISTIANSEN, J.S. Three years growth hormone treatment in growth hormone deficient adults: normalization of body composition and physical performance. European Journal of Endocrinology, 130, 224-8. 1994.

JORGENSEN, J.O.L., et al. Growth hormone versus placebo treatment for one year in growth hormone deficient adults: increase in exercise capacity and normalization of body composition. Clinical Endocrinology 45:681-688. 1996.

KLITGAARD, H., MANTONI, M., SCHIAFFINO, S., et al. Function, morphology and protein expression of aging skeletal muscle: a cross-sectional study of elderly men with different backgrounds. Acta Physiology of Scandinavia. 140:41-54, 1990.

KOJIMA, M., et al. Ghrelin is a growth hormone releasing accylated peptide from stomach. Nature. Dec 9;402(6762):656-60. 1999.

LANGE, K.H.W., ANDERSEN, J.L., BEYER, N., ISAKSSON, F., LARSSON, B., HØJBY, M., RASMUSSEN, JUUL, A., BÜLOW, J., AND KJÆR, M. GH administration changes myosin heavy chain isoforms in skeletal muscle but does not augment muscle strength or hypertrophy, either alone or combined with resistance exercise training in healthy elderly men. The Journal of Clinical Endocrinology and Metabolism Vol. 87, No. 2 513-523. 2002.

LARSSON, L. Morphological and functional characteristics of the aging human skeletal muscle in man. Acta Physiology Scandinavia. 140:41-54, 1990.

LEXELL, J., Aging and human skeletal muscle: observations from Sweden. Canadian Journal of Applied Physiology. 18:2-18, 1993.

LEXELL, J.D., TAYLOR, C.C., SJOSTROM, M. What is the cause of the aging atrophy? Total number, size, and proportion of different fiber types studied in whole vastus lateralis muscle from 15-83 year old men. Journal of Neurology and Science. 84:275-294, 1988.

MCGAULEY, G.A., Quality of life assessment before and after growth hormone treatment in adults with growth hormone deficiency. Acta Paediatric Scandinavia Supplement. 356:70-72; discussion 73-74. 1989.

MCGAULEY GA, CUNEO RC, SALOMON F et al. Psychological Well-Being Before and After Growth Hormone Treatment in Adults with Growth Hormone Deficiency. Hormone Research. ;33 (suppl 4):52-54. 1990.

MCKENNA, S.P., & DOWARD, L.C. What is the impact of GH deficiency and GH replacement on quality of life in childhood-onset and adult-onset GH deficiency. In Monson ed. Challenges in growth hormone therapy. Oxford: Blackwell Science;160-176. 1999.

MORGANTI, C.M., NELSON, M.E., FIATARONE, M.A. Strength improvements with one year of progressive resistance training in older women. Medicine and Science in Sports and Exercise. 1995.

MULLER. E.E., GH-related and extra endocrine actions of GH secretagogues in aging. Neurobiological Aging Sep-Oct;23(5):907-19. 2002.

NEWMAN, A.B., HAGGERTY, C.L., GOODPASTER, B., HARRIS, T., KRITCHEVSKY, S., NEVITT, M., MILES, T.P., AND VISSER, M. (Health, Aging, and Body Composition Research Group). Strength and Muscle Quality in a Well-Functioning Cohort of Older Adults: The Health, Aging and Body Composition Study. Journal of the American Geriatrics Society 51:3 323 1532-5415. 2002.

O'HALLORAN DJ, TSATSOULIS A, WHITEHOUSE RW et al. Increased Bone Density after Recombinant Human Growth Hormone (GH) Therapy in Adults with Isolated GH Deficiency. Journal of Clinical Endocrinology and Metabolism;76:1344-1348. 1993.

ORME, S.M., SABASTIAN, J.P. OLDROYD, B., STEWART, S.P., GRANT, P.J., STRICKLAND, M.H., SMITH, M.A. & BELCHETZ, P.E. Comparison of measures of body composition in a trial of low dose growth hormone replacement therapy. Clinical Endocrinology, 37, 453-9. 1992.

PAFFENBARGER, R.S JR, HYDE R.T., WING A.L., HSIEH C.C. Physical activity, all-cause mortality, and longevity of college alumni. New England Journal of Medicine;314:605-13. 1986.

PALLI D., KROGH V., RUSSO A., BERRINO F., PANICO S., TUMINO R., VINEIS P. EPIC-Italy. A molecular epidemiology project on diet and cancer. Advanced Exp Medical Biology; 472:21-8. 1999.

ROBINSON, B.M., et al. Acute Growth hormone (GH) response to GH-releasing hexapeptide in humans independent of endogenous GH-releasing hormone. Journal of Clinical Endocrinology and Metabolism, vol. 75 No. 4;1121-4343. 1992.

RODGERS, M.A., and EVANS, W.J. Changes in skeletal muscle with aging effects of exercise training. Exercise and Sports Science Review. 21:65-102, 1993.

RODGERS, M.A., HAGBERG, J.M., MARTIN, W.H., EHSAHI, A.A., HOLLOSZY, J.O. Decline in VO2max with aging in master athletes and sedentary men. Journal of Applied Physiology. 68:2195-2199, 1990

ROIZEN, M. Real Age: Are You as Young as You Can Be?: HarperCollins. 1999.

ROOT, A.W., AND ROOT, M.J. Clinical pharmacology of human growth hormone and its secretagogues. Current Drug Targets Immune Endocrinonology Metabolic Disorders. Apr;2(1);27-52. 2002.

ROSEN, T.G., JOHANNSSON, JOHANNSSON, BENGTSSON. Consequences of growth hormone deficiency in adults and the benefits and risks of recombinant human growth hormone treatment. Hormone Research 43:93-99. 1995.

ROSICKA, M., et al. Ghrelin – a new endogenous growth hormone secretagogue. Physiological Research; 51(5):435-41. 2002.

RUDMAN D., FELLER A.G., NAGRAJ H.S., et al. Effects of human growth hormone in men over 60 years old. New England Journal of Medicine. 323:1–6. 1990.

RUTHERFORD, O.M., JONES, D.A., ROUND, J.M., BUCHANAN, C.R., & PREECE, M.A. Changes in skeletal muscle and body composition after discontinuation of growth hormone treatment in growth hormone deficient young adults. Clinical Endocrinology, 34, 469-75. 1991.

RUTHERFORD, O.M., BESHYAH, S.A. & JOHNSTON, D.G. Quadriceps strengths before and after growth hormone replacement in hypo-pituitary adults: relationship to changes in lean body mass and IGF-I. Endocrinology and Metabolism, 1, 41-7. 1994.

SALOMON F., CUNEO R.C., HESP R., SORKSEN P.T.H. The effects of treatment with recombinant human growth hormone on body composition and metabolism in adults with growth hormone deficiency. New England Journal of Medicine; 321:1797-1803. 1989.

SHUTO, Y., SHIBASAKI, T. Hypothalamic growth hormone secretagogue receptor regulates growth hormone secretion, feeding and adiposity. Journal of Clinical Investigations. June;109. 2002.

SKELTON, D.A., AND DINAN, S.M. Exercise and falls management: Rationale for an exercise program to reduce postural instability. Physiotherapy: Theory and Practice. 15:105-120. 1999.

SKELTON, D.A., GRIEG, C., DAVIES, J. AND YOUNG, A. Strength, power and related functional ability of healthy people aged 65-89 years. Age Aging, 23:371-377. 1994.

SKELTON, D.A., YOUNG, A., WALKER, A. AND HOINVILLE, E. Physical activity in later life – Further analysis of the Allied Dunbar National Fitness Survey and the Health Education Authority Survey of Activity and Health. Health Education Authority, London, 1999.

SMITH R.G., CHENG K., SCHOEN W.R., et al. A nonpeptidyl growth hormone secretagogue. Science. 260:1640–1643. 1993.

SPIRDUSO, W. Physical Dimensions of Aging. Human Kinetics, Champaign, Illinois. 1995.

SUTTON-TYRRELL, K., NEWMAN, A., SIMONSICK, E.M., HAVLIK, R., PAHOR, M., LAKATTA, E., SPURGEON, H., AND VAITKEVICIUS, P. Aortic stiffness is associated with visceral adiposity in older adults enrolled in the study of health, aging, and body composition,

Hypertension. Sep;38(3):429-33. 2001.

SVENSSON, J., STIBRANT SUNNERHAGEN, K., AND JOHANNSSON, G. Five Years of Growth Hormone Replacement Therapy in Adults: Age- and Gender-Related Changes in Isometric and Isokinetic Muscle Strength. The Journal of Clinical Endocrinology and Metabolism,Vol. 88, No. 5 2061-2069. 2003.

SVENSSON, L., LÖNN, J.-O., JANSSON, G., MURPHY, D., WYSS, D., KRUPA, K., CERCHIO, W., POLVINO, B., GERTZ, B.J., BOSEAUS, L., SJÖSTRÖM L., BENGTSSON, B.A. Two-Month Treatment of Obese Subjects with the Oral Growth Hormone (GH) Secretagogue MK-677 Increases GH Secretion, Fat-Free Mass, and Energy Expenditure, The Journal of Clinical Endocrinology and Metabolism Vol. 83, No. 2 362-369. 2002.

TINETTI, M., DOUCETTE, J., CLAUS, E. AND MAROTOLLI, R. Risk factors and serious injury during falls for older persons in the community. Journal of the American Geriatrics Society. 45:1214-1221. 1995.

TOOGOOD, A.A., ADAMS, J.E., O'NEILL, P.A. & SHALET, S.M. Body composition in growth hormone deficient adults over the age of 60 years. Clinical Endocrinology, 45, 399-405. 1996.

TORNVALL, G. Assessment of physical capabilities. Acta Physiologica Scandinavia 53 (Suppl. 210) 1-102. 1963.

VAHL, N., JORGENSEN, J.O.L., JURIK, A.G. & CHRISTIANSEN, J.S. Abdominal adiposity and physical fitness are major derminants of the age associated decline in stimulated GH secretion in healthy adults. Journal of Clinical Endocrinology and Metabolism, 81, 2209-15. 1996.

VAHL, N., JORGENSEN, J.O.L., SKJAERBAEK, C., VELDHUIS, J.D., ORSKOV, H. & CHRIS-TIANSEN, J.S. Abdominal adiposity rather than age and sex predicts mass and regularity of GH secretion in healthy adults. American Journal of Physiology, 272, E1108-16. 1997.

WEITS, T., VAN DER BEEK, E.J., WEDEL, M., & TER HAAR ROMENY, B.M. Computed tomography measurement of abdominal fat deposition in relation to anthropometry. International Journal of Obesity, 12, 217-225. 1988.

WHITEHEAD, H.M., BOREHAM, C., MCILRATH, E.M., SHERIDAN, B., KENNEDY, L., ATKIN-SON, A.B. & HADDEN, D. R. Growth hormone treatment of adults with growth hormone deficiency: results of a 13-month placebo controlled cross-over study. Clinical Endocrinology, 36, 45-52. 1992.

WREN. A.M., et al. The hypothalamic mechanisms of the hypophysiotropic action of ghrelin. Neuroendocrinology Nov;76(5):3116-24. 2002.

YOUNG, D. AND DINAN. Active in later life. In ABC of Sports Medicine. British Medical Journal Books. 2000.

Participants reported changes in study and control group (blank spaces indicate no noticed changes)

Participant	Increased energy	Improved sleep	Felt leaner	Other changes noted
P1				
P2	Did not complete study			
P3				
P4				
P5				
P6	Did not complete study			
P7				
P8				
P9				
P10				
P11	Did not complete study			
P12				Improved skin condition
P13				
P14	Did not complete study			
S1	Yes	Yes		Improved mood
S2	Yes	Yes	Yes	Hospital test revealed 0 fat reading in liver, improved mood
S3	Did not complete study			
S4				
S5				Felt fitter, lower cholesterol reading
S6	Yes	Yes	Yes	Less aches and pains, increased energy almost immediately, increased stamina, improved mood
S7	Yes		Yes	Improved muscle tone on face and legs, after a week on the supplement menstrual cycle restarted, hair condition improved
S8	Yes			Improved muscle tone
S9	Did not complete study			
S10				
S11	Yes	Yes		Hot flashes stopped, felt more aches and pains
S12			Yes	Improved muscle tone in arms
S13	Yes	Yes	Yes	Increased stamina, improved muscle tone, elevated mood
S14	Yes	Yes	Yes	Increased libido, improved muscle tone